The New York Times

GUIDE TO SIMPLE HOME REPAIRS

BY BERNARD GLADSTONE

A & W VISUAL LIBRARY

Contents

CHAPTER I

TOOLS AND MATERIALS

It would be virtually impossible for anyone to make up a really complete list of all the tools and materials that everyone should have on hand in order to meet all household emergencies—so some people recommend adopting a policy of not buying *any* tools or materials until the need for them actually arises. This may be one way to avoid spending a lot of money on an over-large assortment of tools, but if carried to the extreme it means that you will be forever running to the local hardware store—and you are bound to get stuck in the middle of a job on some weekend or evening when all the stores in the neighborhood are closed.

Actually, the wisest policy is to follow a somewhat middle course—that is, assemble a basic assortment of good quality hand tools and frequently used supplies that almost everyone will need at one time or another, then add to these as you gain experience and the need for other tools arises. Bearing this in mind, this chapter will list tools which should be included in every woman's basic assortment, along with some pointers on selecting and working with each of them.

When buying your tools, remember that even the best quality hand tools are comparatively inexpensive and in normal use will probably last a lifetime, so it is foolish economy to buy only those of "bargain basement" quality. Cheap tools will not only need replacing more often, they also will make every job much harder and more tedious to complete—and in many cases they are also more likely to be a cause of accidents (blades break, handles come off and jaws slip). This list is by no means all-inclusive, but it should prove a good starting point for every handywoman.

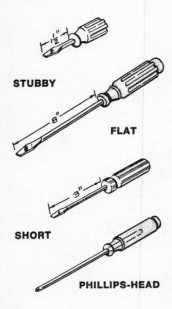

Figure 1: Screwdrivers.

Screwdrivers

You'll need at least three, and preferably four, screwdrivers (see figure 1). The first two should be of the conventional flat blade type—one medium size and one small—the third should be a cross-slot or Phillips type since screws with cross-slot heads are often used by manufacturers in assembling appliances, furniture, and other items which you may have occasion to take apart or repair.

These three will probably handle 90 percent of your work, but there is one other type that you will occasionally need and that will be literally "worth its weight in gold" when the need for it does occur: this is a short screwdriver usually referred to as a "stubby" model. It will enable you to reach into many tight places where a conventional long-handled screwdriver would not fit—for example, reaching between shelves which are close together or reaching under a short-legged piece of furniture when you want to tighten a screw on the underside. Stubby screwdrivers come in various widths and in both Phillips and regular types, but as a start, one medium size, flat-blade, stubby driver will probably solve most of your problems.

Pliers

If you want to keep your tool collection to a bare minimum, then you can probably get by with just one pair of pliers—a pair of slip-joint pliers similar to the ones illustrated here. It should have jaws that meet smoothly with a minimum of excess play in the pivot joint. The slip-joint enables you to shift the relative position of the handles so that the pliers will open to grab large diameter objects, although in this position its grip won't be quite as strong. Some models have built-in wire cutters, which can come in handy on many jobs. (See figure 2.)

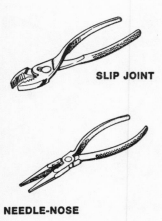

Figure 2: Pliers.

In addition to a pair of slip-joint pliers (6 to 8 inches in length) you'll also find a pair of needle-nose pliers invaluable for many jobs where you have to reach into tight corners, particularly when doing electrical work. They're also handy for holding small nails and brads while starting them (to avoid mashing your fingers), as well as for many other jobs where an ordinary pair of pliers will not fit. For maximum versatility, buy a pair that also has built-in wire cutters since this will be extremely handy when doing electrical work. You can use the pointy nose for bending the end of a wire into a loop to fit around terminal screws, while the built-in cutter will enable you to do a neat job of snipping off excess wire.

Hammers

You'll probably need only one of these for most of your repair jobs around the home—a carpenter's claw hammer of medium size and weight (10 ounces is a good size, see figure 3). However, make the one hammer that you buy a good one; it should be nicely balanced with a polished steel head to minimize the possibility of accidentally bending nails or banging a finger—on a good hammer the head is less likely to slide off the top of a nail if your blow is not dead center. Also, the claws will have sharp ends and inside edges so that it will be easier to pull out nails even when the head is almost flush with the surface.

Figure 3: **Claw hammer.**

Wrenches

As a bare minimum you'll need at least two different kinds of wrenches—one adjustable wrench similar to the one shown (4a) for loosening or tightening nuts or bolts, and one pipe wrench for plumbing jobs to grip pipes and other round objects (see figure 4b).

The adjustable Crescent-type wrench (Crescent is actually the brand name of the manufacturer who first produced this type of wrench) should be about 8 inches long if you're going to own only one (see figure 4a). However, you'll soon find that there are many jobs where you need two wrenches—one to hold a bolt head at one end and another to tighten a nut at the other end. If you're going to buy two, then buy two different sizes; one 8 or 10 inches long and one 6-inch model so that you can also use it on smaller jobs. Better yet, buy one adjustable wrench (8-inch) and a set of open-end or box wrenches (see figure 5). These are comparatively inexpensive but they will enable you to get a firm grip without worrying about the adjustment working

Figure 4a: **Adjustable Crescent wrench.**

Figure 4b: **Pipe wrench.**

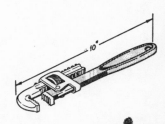

Figure 5: **Combination open-end and box wrench.**

loose, and they will also reach into places where an adjustable wrench will not fit. A set that contains double-ended wrenches (an opening at each end) and that will handle nuts from ¼ to ¾ inch in diameter can be purchased for only a few dollars and will prove invaluable on many repair jobs.

A pipe wrench has two serrated jaws—one fixed and one movable—and it is specifically designed to grip round objects firmly. For most repair jobs around the home, one wrench 8 or 10 inches in length will do the trick.

There is one other type of exceptionally versatile wrench which is really not a wrench at all—it is a cross between a wrench and a pair of pliers and it has unlimited uses that overlap the functions of both these tools. Usually referred to as a locking pliers, it is, as its name implies, very much like a pair of pliers in appearance (see figure 6). However, a compound lever mechanism enables you to close the jaws with a powerful grip many times stronger than you could apply by hand and also keeps it locked onto the work so that you can use it as a portable vise, a twisting tool, or a clamp—as well as in place of a pipe wrench, adjustable wrench, or conventional pair of pliers. Most brands also have powerful wire cutters built in that are strong enough so that by gradually increasing the pressure on the jaws (there is an adjustable screw that enables you to do this with very little effort) you can actually cut small bolts and large nails, as well as the heaviest wires. Even if you've never seen one of these tools, experience has proven that once you use one you will never again want to be without it.

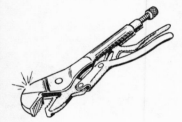

Figure 6: **Vise-grip pliers.**

Saws

If you're only interested in those repairs that are absolutely necessary, then chances are you won't need a full-size carpenter's saw—but you will need a small saw for trimming moldings or occasionally cutting metal. Your best bet for work of this kind is to buy an all-purpose utility saw similar to the one pictured here (see figure 7). This consists of a single handle with two or three interchangeable blades, one of which is usually a metal cutting blade. The other two

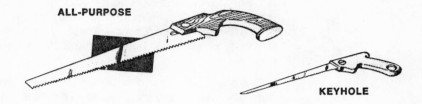

ALL-PURPOSE

KEYHOLE

Figure 7: Saws.

are for cutting wood—one smaller and more pointed with fine teeth for cutting curves and inside openings, the other larger and coarser for conventional wood cutting. As you become more experienced and undertake more ambitious projects, you may find it advisable to buy a regular crosscut saw and eventually, perhaps, a metal-cutting hacksaw (see figure 8).

Wood Chisels

There are many jobs, such as installing or resetting hinges on doors, where the only tool that will do the required trimming and shaping is a wood chisel. To begin with you can probably get by with just one size; a chisel that is ½ inch wide; however, if at all possible it's advisable to buy one of the handy sets that are available in most well-stocked hardware stores. These will include three or four chisels that vary from ¼ to 1 inch in width (see figure 9) and as an added plus they usually come in a handy pocket pouch which keeps them all neatly together and protects the sharp edges against accidental nicking or damage (and also protects your fingers when you reach into a drawer or box in which the chisels are stored).

Planes

A wood plane is used for trimming door edges, moldings, and other wood surfaces, as well as for smoothing rough surfaces. Although planes come in many different sizes and styles, initially you should be able to get by with just one small hand plane—

Figure 8: Hacksaw.

Figure 9: Wood Chisels.

Figure 10: **Block plane.**

the type called a block plane (see figure 10). This is a one-hand plane (you hold it with one hand) that will be useful for most of the small trimming jobs you're likely to encounter—unless you intend to tackle jobs such as building cabinets or installing new doors.

In this case you'll need a larger plane of the type normally called a bench plane. This is a two-hand plane which has one handle at the back end and an extra knob or second handle at the front end. The operating principle of all planes is basically the same: a very sharp, chisel-like blade is mounted at an angle so that it projects through the bottom of the plane's base to shave wood as you push it forward over the surface. A good quality plane will hold the blade firmly and will have a blade made of tempered steel that will hold its edge and shave the wood off cleanly with a minimum of effort.

Files

You won't need these tools very often (nor will you need many of them) but when the need for a file does arise nothing else will ever quite do the job.

Files come in many different shapes—square, round, flat, half-round, and triangular—but chances are that one 6- or 8-inch flat file will take care of most of your needs. In addition to varying as to size, files also vary as to coarseness and type of cut (the kind of teeth it has). The teeth on a file slope at an angle across the face and there may be just a single row (single-cut) or a double row (double-cut) which has two rows of teeth crisscrossing each other in opposite directions. Single-cut files give the smoothest finish; double-cut files cut faster but do not leave as smooth a surface.

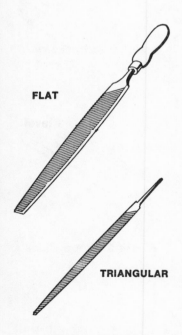

FLAT

TRIANGULAR

Figure 11: **Files.**

Since the only time you'll require a file for average repairs around the house is for smoothing off a rough edge on a piece of metal, chances are that all you'll need is a combination file which has single-cut teeth on one side and double-cut teeth on the other (see figure 11). In addition, a small triangular file will come in handy for reaching into tight spots where a conventional flat file won't fit, as well as for marking grooves when starting cuts with a metal cutting saw. Files will also be needed for sharpening many yard and garden tools such as rotary lawn mower blades, small hatchets, hoes, edgers, and similar tools.

Measuring and Leveling Tools

Of the many different kinds of rulers available for home use, you'll probably find flexible steel tapes the most convenient. These come in various sizes that extend anywhere from 8 to 50 feet, but for your work around the house you'll find a 12-foot steel tape the most useful (see figure 12). It is long enough to handle most measuring jobs with a single length, yet compact and light enough to be carried around easily. The newest models have plastic-covered faces that stay clean and are rust-resistant and they are rigid enough when extended so that you can reach upward for several feet without having the ruler fold back on you.

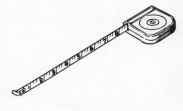

Figure 12: **Flexible tape.**

A good yardstick will also come in handy—for measuring and to serve as a straightedge. In addition, if you're going to tackle projects such as putting up shelves or building cabinets, you'll find a 24-inch bubble level handy (see figure 13). This is not only used for telling when horizontal surfaces are level, it also enables you to tell when vertical surfaces or edges are plumb and truly vertical (without tilting one way or the other).

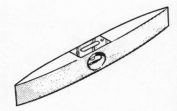

Figure 13: **Bubble level.**

Drills

There are many repair jobs where you'll need some kind of a drill—especially for drilling pilot holes (starting holes) when inserting screws. Chances are that for a large percentage of these you can get by with a simple hand drill—either one of the push-pull types (you just pump up and down on the handle to drive the bit into the wood) (see figure 14a) or one of the rotary hand models. However, sooner or later you'll end up wishing you had an electric drill, so your smartest move would be to start out by buying one in the first place. Modern electric drills are surprisingly light, compact, and inexpensive and

Figure 14a: **Push-pull drill.**

Figure 14b: **Electric drill.**

you'll find them handy for a wide variety of jobs—especially as your experience and confidence grows (see figure 14b).

In addition to drilling holes in wood, you can get special bits for drilling in metal, brick, masonry, and ceramic tile; attachments can be added for sanding, buffing, etc. When you go shopping for an electric drill consider spending a few dollars more to buy one of the variable-speed models. With these, the less pressure you apply on the trigger the slower they go. They are very handy for starting holes on hard smooth surfaces (tile, metal, etc.) and they can be equipped with special bits so that you can use them as a power screw driver or nut driver.

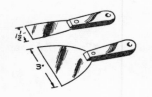

Figure 15: **Putty knives.**

Miscellaneous Tools

In addition to the tools just described, every home repair kit should include a number of other tools which you'll need to meet various emergencies. Among these would be the following:

A sharp utility knife, preferably of the kind that uses disposable blades and stores extra blades in the handle so that you'll always have a sharp one available.

Two putty knives—a stiff one about 1½ or 2 inches wide and another flexible one 3 or 3½ inches in width (see figure 15). The stiff one will be used for various scraping and prying jobs, while the wide, flexible one will be needed for patching cracks and holes in walls and ceilings, as well as for some light-duty scraping jobs.

Figure 16: **Force cup.**

A plumber's force cup—also called a "plumber's friend" or plunger. This is a bell-shaped rubber cup with a handle at the end and it is indispensable for freeing up clogged sinks or toilet drains (see figure 16). It will often save you the price of an expensive visit from the plumber—as well as eliminating the inconvenience of being stuck without sanitary facilities while waiting for the plumber to arrive.

A nail set which, as its name implies, is primarily designed for setting nails (actually nail heads) below the surface of the wood (see figure 17). You'll not only want one of these for various carpentry jobs where you want to recess nail heads so that you can then cover them up with putty, you'll also find a nail set very handy for helping to drive nails in tight corners where a hammer head won't fit or where a poorly aimed blow might cause damage to the surrounding surface.

Taking Care of Your Tools

Regardless of how many of these tools you start out with, chances are that as time passes you'll be adding more. Make an effort to keep all your tools in one place where you can easily find them when needed. You can keep them in a drawer, racked up on wall holders or clips that fit into perforated hardboard, or in one of the many toolboxes that are available from most well-stocked dealers.

The advantage of a portable toolbox or carrier of some kind is that you can pick it up and take it to the job instead of merely carrying a lot of loose tools in your hands or pockets. However, be careful you don't select a box that is too large—when loaded it will be much too heavy for you to carry with ease. You may prefer two smaller boxes rather than one large one; keep the most frequently used tools in one box and those that you'll need only occasionally in the other.

Remember that for working convenience, as well as for safety's sake, all tools should be kept clean and in good repair. A loose or greasy handle on any tool is a hazard because it may slip or you may lose your grip. For the same reason chisels, knives, and other cutting tools should always be sharp since a sharp blade is actually safer to use than a dull one (dull ones require more pressure and slip more readily). If you want to keep them sharp you'll need an oil stone (which you can buy in any hardware store); otherwise most tool dealers can sharpen them.

Figure 17: **Nail set.**

CHAPTER II

PAINTING AND FINISHING

There are more women doing their own painting these days than ever before, not only because good painters are more expensive—and harder to find—but also because modern paints and painting tools have been improved so greatly that there is no reason why any woman cannot accomplish a good-looking paint job.

However, this does not mean that you can just go out and buy any can of good quality paint and be assured of good results. It is true that some brands are advertised as being suitable for practically every purpose, but there is still no such thing as a truly "all-purpose" paint that can be used everywhere and under every condition. That is why most reputable manufacturers make different kinds of paint in a choice of finishes—and why you must know something about the types that are available if you want to get a successful result every time.

Choosing the Right Interior Paint

Interior paints can be divided into four broad categories, depending on their amount of gloss and the uses to which they will be put.

    1. Flat paints have little or no sheen and are used on walls and ceilings. The flat finish makes bumps and wavy areas less obvious, but is also less stain-resistant and will not take as much abuse as paints which dry with a gloss finish.

    2. Semi-gloss paints, also referred to as satin finishes, are midway between high gloss and dead flat when dry. They are used on woodwork such as windows, doors, and trim where you may not want a high-gloss enamel, but do want a finish that is more washable and stain-resistant than a flat. Semi-gloss or satin finishes are also used on walls and

ceilings of kitchens, bathrooms, and laundry rooms of many homes since a semi-gloss stands up better than a flat if exposed to dampness and hard wear. It is less likely to be stained by splashing or accidental spills and will wear longer under repeated scrubbing.

3. High-gloss paints—usually referred to as enamels—give a shiny, hard finish that will take more abuse than the duller finishes. They are generally used on surfaces which get hard wear and are frequently washed—e.g., kitchen cabinets, furniture, toys, and appliances.

4. Primer-sealers or undercoats are designed to be used as a base or primer under the other three finishes. They may be called by various names but are not intended to be used as a finish coat. You need buy one of these only when the manufacturer of the particular paint you plan to use recommends it on his label, or when working on new, previously unpainted surfaces.

You can buy all of these paints in a latex type that thins with water, or in an oil or alkyd type that thins with turpentine or a similar solvent. Chances are that you'll find a latex paint easier and less messy to work with—you can wash your brushes, rollers, or other tools in water or wipe off smears and drips with a damp cloth. You won't need any special thinner since the paint thins with water and you can clean your hands (or clothes) by washing with water—as long as you do it promptly after the job is done. In addition, latex paints dry much faster than oil or alkyd paints so you can replace furniture or apply a second coat, if necessary, within an hour or two. In the flat finishes, latex paints are more stain resistant and tend to cover better than solvent-thinned flat paints.

In spite of the conveniences offered by the use of water-thinned latex paint, there are some places where you still may prefer to use a solvent-thinned paint. This is especially true in the gloss or enamel finishes—you can buy enamels with a latex base, but in most cases really sharp, bright colors are not available and latex enamels still don't cover as well (especially on one-coat jobs) as the alkyd enamels. You must remember that no latex finish will adhere properly over an old gloss or semi-gloss finish—whereas alkyd enamels are less finicky in this respect (although a very shiny surface should be dulled down by sanding or by use of a liquid surface preparer or sanding liquid).

On most repainting jobs around the inside of the house you won't need any special primer or under-coat if you are using a latex paint. If you're painting walls or ceilings where you have just done a great deal of patching—or if there is a drastic color change involved—then a first coat of primer-sealer or under-coat may be advisable (for specific recommenda-tions on this read the label on the paint can). If you're still in doubt, but you're certain that two coats will be required, remember that using an undercoat or primer for the first coat can never hurt. However, these primers come only in white, so if you're going to finish with a dark color you should tint the base coat first—otherwise you'll have quite a time cover-ing with one finish coat.

CHOOSING EXTERIOR PAINTS

Like interior paints, those designed for use around the exterior of your house are now available in latex form, as well as in the older oil or alkyd-base varie-ties. The latex types are easier to work with because you can clean and thin them with water and they spread more easily—so chances are you'll prefer one of these for your outside painting. In addition, exterior latex paints dry much faster than exterior oil paints, so they eliminate several problems—you can put screens and storm sashes back on the same day, you can close windows within an hour or so after painting, you'll have fewer problems with bugs sticking to the wet surface while the paint is still soft, and you can apply two coats on the same day (when and if two coats are required).

Paints used around the outside of the house can be classified into four broad categories: house paints, trim paints, masonry paints and shake or shingle paints.

House paints are those intended for use on clap-board, wood siding, overhanging eaves, and other large areas on the body of the house. Oil base house paints usually have a medium to high gloss, while latex house paints are comparatively dull and dry with a finish that varies from almost flat to a satin sheen.

Trim paints are those intended for use on doors, shutters, windows, and other forms of outdoor trim. They dry to a harder, glossier finish that will take more abuse and sheds dirt more readily. They are usually available in bright, sharp colors you can't find in ordinary house paint. Trim paints should not be used on clapboard or other large surfaces since they dry too hard and are more likely to crack or chip when the wood expands and contracts with seasonal changes in the weather.

Masonry paints are intended for use on brick, stucco, and concrete. They dry to a dull finish and are formulated to be more resistant to attack by excess alkali and moisture (conditions often encountered on masonry).

Shake and shingle paints are very similar to masonry paints in that they also dry dull and are less prone to blistering or peeling when moisture seeps in behind the film (a problem on most masonry and shingle walls). Many companies make one paint that is suitable for use on both masonry and shingles since the problems involved in painting these surfaces are so similar.

As mentioned previously, all of these paints are available in both water-thinned latex types and conventional solvent-thinned oil or alkyd-based formulations. One big advantage offered by most latex exterior paints is that the same paint can be used on three or four different kinds of surfaces. For instance, a latex house paint of good quality is not only suitable for use on clapboard and siding, it is also an excellent masonry and shingle paint. Thus, if your house has more than one kind of exterior surface, instead of having to work with two or three different kinds of paint (if you were using oil paint), one latex paint may be used on almost everything.

In addition to its easy-working and easy-cleanup characteristics, one of the biggest advantages of using a latex exterior paint is that you can safely apply latex over damp surfaces (which means immediately after a rain) as well as during humid weather when oil paint could not be used (in humid weather oil paints do not dry properly, and they often look blotchy when dry). Latex paints are less likely to peel on outside surfaces because they dry with a "breathing" type of film which lets trapped moisture inside the wood or masonry escape harmlessly through the film without causing blisters and eventual peeling. Bear in mind that you get this extra benefit only when you're applying a latex paint over a previously unpainted surface (or one from which the paint has been removed) or directly over another latex paint. However, when you put latex paint over an old oil paint, the old paint can still blister and peel—taking the new paint off with it.

Always remember that outside paints have to stand up under a good deal of exposure and hard wear, so it's foolish economy to buy on the basis of price alone. Choose the best quality you can find and carefully read the manufacturer's instructions on the label describing what primer or undercoat (if any) is required and over what kinds of surfaces the paint can be applied.

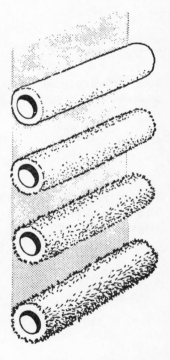

PAINTING WALLS AND CEILINGS

For painting walls, ceilings, and other large flat surfaces, you'll find it easier and faster to use a paint roller rather than a brush. Roller covers are made of different kinds of synthetic fiber with naps or piles of different lengths (see figure 18). Mohair covers, the shortest nap, are used for gloss or semi-gloss finishes, while those with a ¼-inch or ⅜-inch nap are used for conventional flat paint on relatively smooth walls. If your walls have a heavy stipple or other texture, you'll require a longer nap cover—one with fibers that are ½ to ¾ inch in length.

The sequence to follow in painting an entire room is to paint the ceiling first, the walls next, and the woodwork and trim last. Use a 2- or 2½-inch brush to paint the corners and edges where the roller won't reach, completing all the brush work around each wall or ceiling first, then finish the large areas with the roller (see figure 19).

Fill your paint tray about two-thirds full, leaving empty space at the top of the sloping section so you can roll off excess after each dip. Make sure the

Figure 18: Roller covers (from top to bottom) range from mohair for extra-smooth surfaces to ⅜-inch nap for smooth walls to ½-¾-inch nap for textured walls to ½-1½-inch nap for stucco, brick, and very rough surfaces.

Figure 19: **Use brush near windows and in corners.**

roller cover is uniformly saturated to avoid dripping or splattering. When painting walls, make your first stroke with the fully loaded roller in an *upward* direction. On ceilings the first stroke should always be *away* from you. On both walls and ceilings, try to reach as close as possible into each corner so that you cover most of the brushed areas with the roller. To simplify painting your ceilings and to save climbing, buy an extension handle for your roller that will enable you to do the whole job (except for the brushwork in the corners) from the floor.

It is usually best to start applying the paint to the wall with a series of angled strokes so that the pattern forms a large "V" on the surface (see figure 20). Then roll back and forth with parallel strokes to fill in the open spaces and eliminate ridges while spreading the paint uniformly. Bear in mind that for uniform coverage you must apply the paint liberally—especially when working with latex paint—so instead of pressing harder when you start running out of paint, stop and pick up more paint immediately.

PAINTING WOODWORK AND TRIM

Figure 20: **Angle your strokes to form a series of large, overlapping "V"s.**

Although you can use a roller on flush doors and large panels, for most of your other woodwork and trim you'll have to use a conventional paintbrush. Even in the hands of the most skilled painter, an

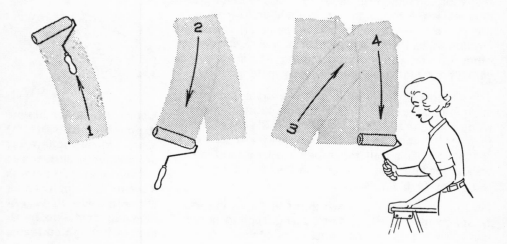

inexpensive, poor quality brush will make it almost impossible to do a good job—so instead of buying cheap "throw-away" brushes which you'll have to replace repeatedly, invest in one or two good brushes which will last for years (see figure 21). Washing them out is no longer the laborious chore it once was since with modern latex paints all you need is plenty of running water. Even with oil paints you can wash your brushes effortlessly if you use one of the liquid brush cleaners designed to emulsify oil paint so that it becomes soluble in water (after you agitate the brush in the liquid you can then wash it out in water).

Another frequent mistake is selecting a paintbrush that is too narrow for the work at hand—either because it costs less than a wider brush or because a narrow one would just fit into the opening in a small can of paint. Actually, for proper and thorough mixing the paint should always be poured out of the original can into a larger pail or bucket (you can buy disposable paper buckets, or save your old coffee cans for this). That way you'll have room to mix without slopping over the sides and be able to dip a brush of adequate size. A wider brush will require fewer brush strokes and will finish the job quicker, with less chance of brush marks or streaks on the surface. As a rule, it is best to choose the widest brush that you can handle easily on the surface being painted—except on very narrow moldings where you're more likely to use the brush edgewise.

A 2-inch sash brush (the kind that has a long handle as pictured in figure 22) will work best on windows, while a 2½- or 3-inch trim brush similar to the one pictured is good for baseboards, door frames, cabinets, and other built-ins. In the 3-inch width this same type of brush is also good for doors—although as you progress you may find that a 3½- or 4-inch brush will get the work done quicker.

When dipping your brush into the paint, never dip it by more than half its bristle length—one-third its length is even better. Dipping your brush deeper than this will only load the heel with paint and will eventually ruin the brush's working qualities, in addition to making it much harder to clean. Apply the

Figure 21: **Flagged tips are one sign of a good brush.**

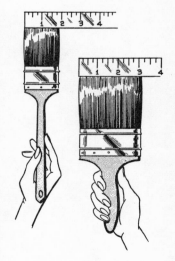

Figure 22: **Left, sash brush; right, trim brush.**

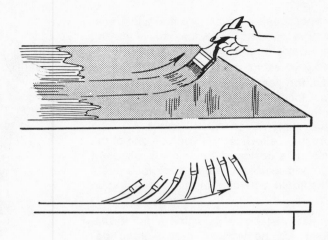

Figure 23: **To leave no brushmarks, paint toward the previously painted area and lift brush gradually at end of each stroke.**

paint with a moderate amount of pressure—but never scrub or rub it on.

Always start on a dry, unpainted area and brush back into the fresh paint. To avoid ridges or visible brush marks try to "feather" each stroke by ending with a gradual lifting action during the final smoothing, making certain you start in a freshly painted section and end up in a previously painted area by lifting up gradually (see figure 23).

PAINTING WINDOWS

Amateur painters seem to have more trouble painting windows than almost any other part of the house, yet with a little practice there is no reason why you can't do a neat job without having to spend hours cleaning paint smears off the glass.

To paint the window moldings and frame without also painting the glass, you can either use one of the various aids or accessories that is available for the purpose or you can learn to "cut in" neatly with the brush the way a skilled professional does.

The most popular accessory for keeping paint off the glass is a metal or plastic shield that looks like a piece of venetian blind slat. You hold it so that its edge is pressed against the molding while you're painting, sliding it along with your brush so that it keeps the bristles from coming into contact with the glass. With one of these gadgets you can do a neat job quickly and easily, but remember, each time you dip the brush into the paint you should also wipe off the edge of the shield with a rag—otherwise accumulated paint will smear onto the glass.

Masking tape provides another method for protecting the glass, but unless it's put on carefully so that the tape does not overlap the wood you may wind up with unpainted edges in some spots. Most people find that putting the tape on accurately takes so long that it's hardly worth the trouble—you might just as well apply the paint as best you can, then scrape off any smears with a razor-blade afterward. If masking tape is used, make sure you pull it off before the paint is completely hard, otherwise you're liable to peel off some of the paint with the tape.

If you have a good quality sash brush with springy bristles that come to a nice sharp edge, there's no reason you can't learn to "cut in" or trim a window neatly by just working free-hand. Dip the brush in no more than 1/3 its bristle length, then tap lightly against the inside rim of the can above the level of the paint. Never wipe your brush across the rim of the can to remove excess since this takes too much paint out and also creates bubbles that make it hard to get a smooth finish—especially when working with varnish (see figure 24).

Figure 24: **Dip bristles only 1/3 their length, then remove excess paint by patting against side of can—NOT by wiping across rim.**

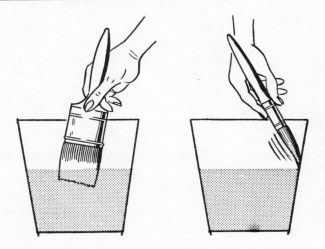

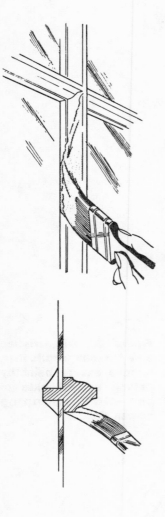

Figure 25: Direct slow, steady stroke toward pane so that bristles fan out and then just touch pane as stroke continues.

Touch the bristles to the wood molding so that they don't actually contact the glass, then press down slightly with a mild twisting action so that the bristles "fan out" to a sharp chisel-like edge. Now move the brush along with a slow but steady stroke while gradually bringing the edge of the bristles up to the glass; then keep moving it along in a straight line with the bristle tips just contacting the glass until the brush starts running out of paint (see figure 25). Stop and pick up more paint before continuing. In each case start out the same way—touch the brush to the wood an inch or so away from the glass, then fan out the bristles and work them in gradually till they touch the glass.

In addition to trying to paint the sash frames without painting the glass, the other problem that usually gives the weekend painter trouble is trying to figure out what sequence to follow—how to paint all parts of both the upper and lower sash frames without skipping and without getting paint all over your hands as you try to move them up and down.

The simplest way to do this is to raise the bottom sash as high as it will go, then lower the top sash as low as it will go. Now, following the sequence illustrated in figure 26, first paint the bottom half of the upper sash as shown, then move the two sashes back to their normal positions—the upper one at the top and the lower one at the bottom, but don't close them all the way—leave each one open about half an inch. Next, finish painting the rest of the upper sash frame, then paint all of the lower sash frame—in each case painting the narrow moldings between the glass first and finishing the outside of each frame last. When you have finished both sashes, paint the window channels and the frame on each side, then the trim around the window, doing the window sill last.

WORKING WITH VARNISH AND ENAMEL

Varnishes and enamels are similar in composition, the main difference being that varnish is clear while enamel has pigment added to give it color and make it opaque. Since they are both applied on fur-

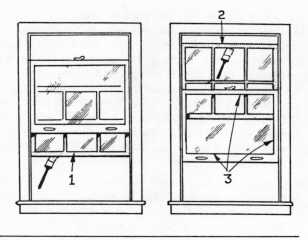

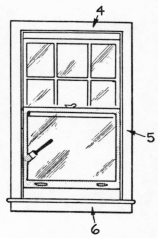

niture, cabinets, and similar surfaces where you want an extra-smooth finish, you should expect to spend a little more time and care in applying them.

Varnish is transparent, so you'll have to be especially careful in preparing the wood underneath because every flaw will show up through the finish. Thorough sanding is necessary to remove stains and blemishes. Always finish with a very fine grit to remove all scratches left by the coarser grades of sandpaper.

A clean surface is a must for a smooth finish with varnish or enamel since dust left on the surface will inevitably result in a rough-looking "sandy" finish. This means you should be especially careful about dusting and cleaning the wood. One way is to use a vacuum cleaner, then a cloth moistened with paint thinner. Better yet, wipe with a special tacky cloth (usually called a tack rag) that is available in most well-stocked paint stores.

For a smooth finish you'll also need a good quality, fully stocked brush with plenty of flagged bristles (see drawing on page 19). Dip the brush into the varnish or enamel no more than one-third its bristle length, then flow the varnish or enamel on liberally with only a slight amount of pressure on the brush. Ideally, you should first apply the finish with short strokes that go across the grain, then lightly with long strokes parallel to the grain.

Figure 26: **Paint the two sash frames as indicated, following the window positions from left to right. Shaded areas indicate where paint has been applied.**

As you dip the brush into the can each time, remember *not* to wipe the excess off by dragging the bristles across the rim. Instead, tap the bristle tips lightly against the inside of the container above the surface of the liquid to remove the excess. The idea is to remove no more paint than necessary to prevent dripping as you carry the brush to the work (see figure 24). You also make air bubbles by pressing too heavily on the brush or by an excessive amount of back-and-forth brushing. That's why it is so important to brush lightly with long strokes.

Wherever possible when finishing furniture or small pieces, try to lay the surface on which you are working in a horizontal position. If you have to work on vertical surfaces, start by brushing across (horizontally), then cross-stroke vertically to eliminate brush marks and spread the finish out uniformly. Keep checking back every few minutes to make certain that no sags or runs have developed—if any are noticed, brush them out immediately before the paint gets too tacky to permit smoothing.

On furniture or cabinets always remove all hardware before starting since it's almost impossible to do a neat job of brushing around obstructions of this kind. Chests or cabinets with drawers are best painted by taking the drawers out and standing them up so that the front is horizontal. If more than one coat will be required (with either varnish or glossy enamel) thin the first coat with about 10 percent paint thinner, then put the second coat on as it comes from the can. In each case, allow the finish to dry completely hard, then sand lightly with very fine sandpaper between coats. After sanding, don't forget to remove all the dust before you brush on the next coat.

When buying varnish or enamel, remember that these finishes come in varying degrees of semi-gloss or satin gloss, as well as in the traditional high gloss. The semi-gloss finishes save you the job of rubbing down a high gloss on surfaces where you don't want a shiny finish, but are not quite as durable as the high-gloss finishes. In addition, if you are painting or varnishing something that will be used outdoors or exposed to the weather, then chances are you'll have to use a high gloss—few, if any, of the semi-gloss varnishes or enamels are suitable for exterior use. The working techniques are, however, similar in each case.

USING WOOD STAINS

A wood stain is more like a dye than a paint or finish—it is designed to soak into the wood and change its color without hiding the original texture or grain. A wood stain either may have a latex or an oil base but with one or two exceptions it is not a finish—it is merely a means for coloring the wood before you apply a clear finish over it (varnish, shellac, lacquer, etc.). The one or two exceptions are some of the wood sealers or transparent wood finishes that are available with pigment or color added. They are made with either a wax base or a special hard (processed) oil base and come in either clear (no color added) or pigmented form (with color added). In either case these are penetrating finishes which soak into the wood so that they leave little or no surface film and just a slight amount of gloss.

Unlike a varnish that stays on the wood's surface, penetrating sealers and finishes soak into the fibers, so there really is no surface film to scratch—although this does not mean that the wood cannot be scratched. Penetrating finishes of this kind are popular on floors where you want a dark finish without having to worry about a lot of scratches showing up, as well as on furniture and shelving where many prefer a low-luster "oiled" type of finish, rather than the built-up look of a varnish finish.

When you go shopping for any type of wood stain—regardless of whether it's a stain–sealer, a penetrating finish, or an ordinary oil stain over which you will later apply varnish or shellac—remember that, unlike paint, the color samples that you see in the store are not necessarily an accurate indication of the color you will get on the wood in your home. Paints are opaque (as long as you apply enough coats to cover completely) so the color underneath has no effect on the finished color and the color you see on the sample in the store is exactly what you should get at home.

However, wood stains are transparent, so the color of the wood underneath will affect the finished color of the stain. If your wood is redder than the wood used for the sample, then the finished effect will be redder than you expected. By the same token, lighter woods will come out lighter and darker woods will come out darker, so the only sure way to know what color you will get is to try a sample first on exactly the same kind of wood—or on an inconspicuous corner of the actual piece being worked on.

Since wood stains must soak into the surface, the porosity of the wood will also affect the color—soft, porous woods come out darker, while harder woods generally come out lighter (the stain doesn't soak in as much). Cheap grades of wood with uneven porosity and sappy streaks will, therefore, come out uneven or blotchy. One way to prevent this, when you have to stain soft wood, is to apply a thin coat of clear penetrating sealer before the stain. Thin the sealer with about 10 to 20 percent turpentine, then apply it uniformly over the wood and allow to dry before staining. If the wood feels fuzzy, sand *very lightly* with very fine sandpaper and dust thoroughly before applying the stain. If done properly, this technique partially seals a porous wood enough so that the stain will "take" uniformly without soaking in excessively and without creating the blotchy appearance that often results when an inferior grade of wood is stained.

USING SPRAY PAINTS

Aerosol paints in spray cans are now available in almost every kind of finish—flat, enamel, stain, varnish, lacquer, and shellac—and in a tremendous variety of colors, shades, and materials. You can also buy aerosol-powered spray units that let you "make your own" spray can. These consist of an aerosol spray can with nothing in it but the gas that supplies the power. It is attached to an atomizer-type sprayer that has a small glass jar into which you can pour any paint in your own choice of finish and color—you'll usually have to thin it to some extent to make it spray properly. You can clean out the glass jar when you're finished and reuse it by buying refills for the aerosol power.

Aerosol spray paints are ideal for many small jobs and for use on hard-to-paint surfaces such as grillwork, wicker, or wrought iron. However, if you want to avoid disappointment remember that spray paints do have their limitations and work best on small surfaces—it's tough to get a professional-looking job on a large flat area with a spray can.

Here are some other pointers that will help ensure good results when using an aerosol-packed spray paint.

1. Shake the can thoroughly before each use. Unless it is a clear finish, it should have a metal ball on the inside to act as an agitator. If you don't hear this ball rattling around on the inside when you shake the can, try tapping the bottom hard against a solid surface to dislodge the ball, then shake again.

2. The surface you are painting should be clean and dry and free of all wax, oil, grease, dirt, and peeling paint. Spraying over a dirty surface may keep the paint from drying or sticking properly and spraying over a previously peeling surface will only make the condition worse.

3. If you're spraying over a previously painted surface, always test first in an inconspicuous corner—especially if you're spraying with a lacquer. This is to ensure that the new finish will not "lift" or blister the old finish. If it dries smooth and hard, then you know it's safe to go ahead with the whole job.

4. Hold the spray can about 8 to 10 inches from the surface and move it so that the nozzle is always at a constant distance from the work (see figure 27). Never swing your arm in an arc since this will bring the can closer to the work at the center of the stroke and will result in uneven coverage.

5. Don't hold the spray can in one place too long and avoid spraying on too much at one time. Two thin coats are always better than one heavy one when spraying, but allow the first coat to dry before applying the second. This will minimize the problem many people have with paint running or dripping because too much has been applied.

6. If you use only part of the spray can, you can keep the nozzle from clogging by turning the can upside down and then spraying out any paint that remains in the tube or nozzle. After a second or two, only gas will come out, then all you have to do is wipe the nozzle tip off to remove any paint from the opening.

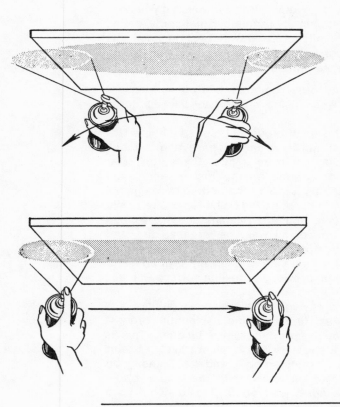

Figure 27: **Don't wave spray-paint can in an arc. Rather, spray straight across.**

7. Always keep the can moving as long as you've got your finger on the button. Holding it in one place too long will cause the paint to build up too fast and will result in drips and runs.

8. Plan your work so that excess spray will not be able to settle onto surfaces that are already finished. On a horizontal table top, for example, start spraying the part that is closest to you, then work away from yourself. In this way excess spray will not settle onto a previously painted surface—often the cause of a gritty, textured finish instead of the smooth one that was expected.

9. Spray tends to travel and drift, so try to move the work into an area (basement or garage) where flying spray won't damage anything, or cover the floor and surroundings with an inexpensive plastic drop cloth, old newspapers, or rags. If you work outdoors, make certain there is no breeze.

USING PAINT AND VARNISH REMOVERS

On many of your painting and refinishing jobs around the house you'll find that you first must remove all of the old finish—in some cases because the old paint is badly checked, blistered, or peeling; in others because you want to get down to the original wood so that you can apply a stain or other natural wood finish. You can perform this task in one of three ways: by scraping the old finish off with a hand scraper; by sanding it off with an electric sander; or by using a prepared chemical paint and varnish remover.

Hand scraping is by far the hardest of the three methods and it is only practical for taking off small patches of peeling paint where the finish is already loose and flaky. Sanding with an electric machine is easier and faster than scraping if you use a disk or belt sander. However, disk sanders should only be used for comparatively rough work around the outside of your house because disks tend to gouge the surface and leave whirl marks—they should never be used on furniture or interior paneling. A belt sander will work fast and leave a smooth finish but these machines are rather heavy to handle, especially when working on vertical surfaces or overhead. (Both belt sanders and disk sanders can usually be rented from local hardware stores or tool rental agencies.)

Prepared chemical removers, which are available in all paint and hardware stores, are the easiest method for removing old paint and varnish—although on a sizable job it may cost you more than sanding would. There are a variety of removers you can buy, but all are designed to work in the same manner—when you spread them over an old finish they soften up the paint or varnish so that you can easily scrape or wash it off.

Removers come either in liquid form or in what is referred to as a semi-paste—the latter has a much thicker consistency, something like heavy cream. Liquids are cheaper, but they will run off vertical surfaces before they can do their job of softening the old finish. In addition, a liquid remover is more volatile and evaporates more quickly, so you'll need more of it to do the same job. Since a remover only works until the solvents in it evaporate, liquids do not penetrate as thoroughly as semi-pastes when applied over heavy coats of finish.

Another reason why semi-paste removers are generally more effective is because they can be applied in thicker layers and stay wet longer—hence they keep on working longer. Special ingredients that are added to thicken the solution so it won't run also form a film over the surface that keeps the air away and retards evaporation—thus giving the solvents in the remover more time to do their work. In the "older" forms of remover these added ingredients have a wax base that leaves a residue on the surface which must be neutralized or washed off with paint thinner or similar solvent before a new finish can be applied. To eliminate the need for this, many of the newer removers are of the so-called "no-wash" type—they do not contain wax and need no after-rinse.

The newest addition to the field is the water-wash type. This is a remover that contains special emulsifiers so that you can wash it off with water. Not only does this eliminate the need for washing with paint thinner, it also permits you to flush off the softened old finish with water—a lot simpler and quicker than scraping it off.

This water-wash feature is particularly handy when you are working on carved or grooved surfaces—all of the softened finish can be washed off by simply scrubbing with a stiff brush dipped into water or by flushing the finish off under a faucet or with a hose. In most cases these methods will leave a cleaner surface than you get by scraping, but remember you have to be careful on old furniture because water might harm the glued joints or loosen the veneer.

Chemical removers also vary as to combustibility. Originally they were all highly inflammable, but some of the newer formulations are now nonflammable. These cost more but are much safer to use indoors—particularly if there is likely to be an open flame nearby or if anyone may be smoking.

Regardless of the kind of remover you choose, remember that it should only be used in a well-ventilated room (unless you're working outdoors) and you should wear plastic gloves to protect your hands. If any of the chemical accidentally gets splashed onto your skin, wash it off immediately. If you have to work overhead, or if you are going to work where there is a chance of splashing, then wear goggles to protect your eyes.

To do its job properly, every remover must be applied liberally and with a minimum of back-and-forth stroking. Once you've brushed it on, don't disturb the finish until it's time to scrape off the softened material. Brushing again or disturbing the film in any way while the remover is working only lets air enter and speeds evaporation of the solvent, thus slowing up or stopping the softening action.

Allow the remover to soak into the finish for anywhere from 15 to 30 minutes (depending on the particular brand being used and on the thickness of the old paint film). Scrape it off with a dull putty knife if the surface is fairly flat, but be careful to avoid scratching the wood (see figure 28). If the surface is not flat, use coarse steel wool or a stiff scrub brush instead of a putty knife. In grooves you can use an old toothbrush or a pointed stick, although with a water-wash remover the simplest method is to scrub with steel wool or a stiff brush while dipping repeatedly in water.

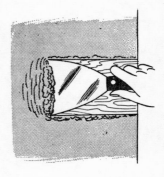

Figure 28: **After old paint soaks in remover, carefully scrape both off with a dull putty knife.**

Ideally, every remover should be put on heavy enough and left on long enough to soften up all of the old finish down to the bare wood in one application. Practically speaking, this doesn't always work, so you'll find it easier to apply a second equally heavy coat directly on top of the first one if the first few scrapes indicate that your old finish is not soft all the way through. Even after doing this, a third—and sometimes a fourth—application may be required in some places to completely remove all of the old finish.

CHAPTER III

WALLS AND CEILINGS

Sooner or later you will find yourself faced with the job of patching small holes and cracks that inevitably seem to develop in the walls or ceilings of most homes and apartments. Sometimes the cause is a settling or warping of the structural beams and other lumber, in other cases there may be holes that are left when you remove pictures, shelves, or lighting fixtures. Regardless of the cause, most cracks and small holes are not especially difficult to patch neatly—although the materials you will need and the techniques involved may vary, depending on whether your walls and ceilings are made of plaster or gypsum wall board (what most people call Sheetrock, which is actually the brand name of just one company's wallboard).

PATCHING PLASTER

Fine cracks and small holes—that is, cracks up to ⅛ inch in width and holes that are not much bigger than a good sized nail—are generally filled with spackling compound. This material will stick in shallow depressions and fine openings where ordinary patching plaster would flake off. It has a smooth, buttery consistency which makes it easy to spread and smooth.

Spackling compound comes in two forms—as a powder which must be mixed with water before use or as a prepared paste which is ready for use from the can. Powdered spackle is slightly cheaper but you'll find the paste type a lot easier to use because you won't have to fuss with mixing or guessing at the right consistency. Paste spackling compounds usually have a vinyl or acrylic base which increases their bonding strength and workability and makes it easier for you to get a smooth finish.

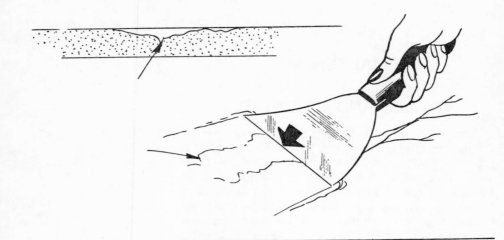

Figure 29: A wide putty knife pressed almost flat will both smooth out the spackle and cause it to fill in properly.

The tool you will need for most spackling jobs is a fairly wide (at least 3 inches) flexible putty knife with a springy blade and a sharp edge that is perfectly straight with no nicks or bends in it. A cheap putty knife will not have the necessary flexibility and will make a smooth finish difficult to get. A putty knife that is too narrow makes it hard to get a smooth patch on long cracks or on sizable holes because it does not bridge a large enough area on the wall. This makes it difficult to "feather out" the compound evenly so that it will blend in smoothly with the surrounding wall surface. A wide, springy blade enables you to press the flat part down against the surface as shown in figure 29, so that you smooth the surface off with the flat of the blade—rather than merely trying to scrape the patch smooth with only the edge of the knife.

Figure 30: To hold plaster, undercut cracks with a sharp tool.

Before filling cracks in a plaster wall, start by cutting the crack out slightly so that you make it wider at the bottom (inside the crack) than it is at the surface. You can use any pointed tool for this, but one of the handiest is an ordinary beverage can opener which has a triangular shaped blade (see figure 30). After you've scraped it out sufficiently to ensure a good mechanical "key" or bond when the patching material is applied, you next dust it out thoroughly with an old paint brush, then dampen the plaster on both sides with clean water.

Scoop a wad of the spackling paste out of the can with your putty knife, then smear it over the crack by wiping it (almost at right angles to the crack) from one side to the other (see figure 31a). After stroking in one direction, make another stroke in exactly the opposite direction—this time pressing harder and trying to squeeze as much material into the opening as possible. In each case press hard enough to cause the blade to curve slightly so that you wipe most of the excess paste off the surface with each stroke.

After crisscrossing strokes several times until the length of the crack is filled and most of the excess compound is scraped off—make a few more strokes almost parallel to, or at a slight angle to, the length of the crack (see figure 31b). This should be done without applying any more material, just working with the dry blade to smooth off the surface of the patch. If done properly, the results should be a smooth finish with little or no compound left on the outside or on the wall at either side of the patch. As a result, very little sanding should be required after it is dry.

Figure 31a: **First wipe putty knife across crack.**

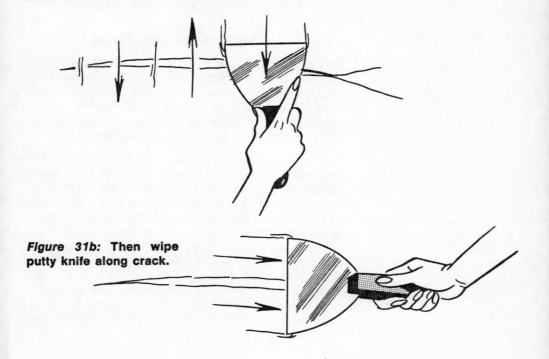

Figure 31b: **Then wipe putty knife along crack.**

Nail holes and other small holes are filled in much the same way—by first smearing the compound in one direction, then crisscrossing strokes until the hole is filled completely flush with little or no excess material left on the surface. With most nail holes the hole itself will be relatively small but extra plaster will be chipped off near the surface so that you may actually have a depression that is an inch or more in width at the surface. This should all be filled at one time, so remember that a wide-blade putty knife is still best for the job—a narrow one might not bridge the depression in one stroke and will tend to leave ridges on the surface, as well as increase the difficulty of achieving a smooth finish.

Spackling compound is also the material to use when you have to fill large shallow patches, as when filling in areas where thick layers of paint have peeled off so that a ridge is left where the old paint still adheres. Smooth the spackle on with the widest putty knife you have, feathering the material out so that the patch blends in smoothly on both sides. Then sand lightly to minimize any rough edges that are left and if necessary apply a second, thinner layer of additional spackling compound.

Larger Cracks and Holes

For larger cracks and holes in plaster—that is, cracks which are more than ¼ inch in width and holes much larger than an ordinary nail hole—you'll have to use patching plaster to fill in most of the depression, after which spackling compound may be used for the final smoothing if needed.

For best results, deep cracks or holes should be patched in two or three layers. The first application should fill it about halfway to the surface, then allow this to harden before filling the rest of the way. This is to minimize the shrinkage which usually occurs when a deep hole is filled with a single application of patching plaster. Start by first chipping away any loose crumbling material around the edges, then wet down the edges of the plaster as well as the lath (the backing over which the plaster was originally applied), if it is exposed, with clean water. Mix your patching plaster to a smooth buttery consistency, then pack it into the depression with a wide putty knife till the crack or hole is filled halfway to the surface.

If the hole is several inches across, you'll find it easier to pack the plaster around the edges first, then gradually work your way into the center until the entire cavity has a layer over the bottom. If the wood or metal lath is exposed, make certain you press the wet plaster tightly against it (after dusting it clean and wetting it) to ensure a good bond for the patch. Make no attempt to smooth off this first layer—instead leave it rough on the surface so that the second coat will bond more securely.

You can apply the next coat of plaster after the first coat has dried completely. Dampen the hardened plaster slightly, then spread on a new layer to bring the patch almost level with the surface. If the hole is more than 3 or 4 inches wide and you can't bridge it smoothly with an ordinary putty knife, you'll need a square metal plasterer's trowel (see figure 32) to do the job. This will bridge a larger area and will make it simpler to smooth the surface of the patch so that it blends in evenly with the surrounding wall. First scoop your freshly mixed plaster out of the pan with a putty knife, using this tool to smear it over the patch, then use your wide trowel to smooth it off.

Since plaster dries fairly quickly (about 10 to 15 minutes), mix no more than you can use up in this amount of time. Once it starts to stiffen, there's no use trying to re-wet it—it'll have to be discarded. To get a smooth glassy finish on the final coat without having the plaster crumble under the trowel as it starts to set, there is a simple trick that all professionals use.

Working rapidly, you first trowel the surface as smooth as possible before the plaster has a chance to stiffen. Then, use a clean brush (a wide paint brush works well) to re-wet the surface of the patch with plain water and drag the trowel over the surface immediately behind the brush. Hold the trowel so that the flat part is against the plaster with its leading edge raised only slightly as indicated in figure 32. As you move it along, bear down hard on the rear

Figure 32: Wetting plaster with brush while troweling.

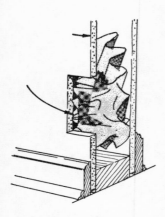

Figure 33: **Pack crumpled paper bag or newspaper through hole into space between walls to be a support for first layer of plaster.**

Figure 34: **Hold heavy metal mesh or corrugated cardboard against wall with string to create backing for plaster.**

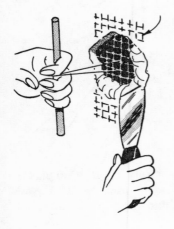

edge and keep the surface wet to keep it from crumbling. After this last layer is completely hard, use spackling compound if necessary to smooth off any depressions or irregularities that remain.

Probably the most annoying type of depression to fill is a so-called "bottomless" hole—one which has no backing at all behind it. You'll have this kind of hole in a wall or ceiling after a light fixture or switch has been moved so that there is a hole that goes all the way through the plaster and lath with nothing behind it except a hollow space. The easiest way to fill this is to stuff in large wads of old newspaper or tightly folded and crumpled cardboard. Push the paper and cardboard in until you've packed in so much that it begins to catch on the back side of the partition or wall (see figure 33). In some cases it may be easier to shove in some crumpled up pieces of wire mesh, then after this has caught in place jam crumpled newspaper on top of it. The idea in either case is to create some sort of backing inside the hole against which a first layer of plaster can be applied.

Another way to create a temporary backing is to use a piece of heavy metal mesh or a piece of corrugated cardboard as shown in figure 34. The piece of mesh or cardboard is cut slightly larger than the hole to be filled, then a piece of string or flexible wire is tied to the middle of it by punching a hole in the center and tying a knot in the back. Push the mesh or cardboard through the hole by bending it slightly to make it fit through the opening, then use the string to pull it up snugly against the back side of the plaster as shown. You can then wrap the string around a pencil or small stick and twist until it holds tightly or you can use a long piece of string to reach a piece of furniture where you can tie it to hold the backing temporarily in place. Cut the string off later—after the hole has been filled with plaster.

After you've "created" a temporary backing for the hole the rest is simple. Pack the plaster in around the edges of the opening so that it grips the old plaster and overlaps onto the paper, cardboard, or mesh. Don't try to fill the entire opening in one application. Instead, pack one layer of plaster around the edges so that it spreads toward the middle for about an inch or so, pushing it in hard enough so that you force it tightly against the backing. Let this dry hard, then repeat with a second and possibly a third layer until you eventually have the entire back of the hole covered and a patch that is level with the surrounding surface. If necessary, a final smoothing coat of spackling compound can be applied after the plaster has dried to fill in any slight depression that may develop when the plaster settles (plaster often shrinks as it dries).

REPAIRING GYPSUM WALLBOARD

Walls and ceilings that are covered with gypsum wallboard (this is known as drywall construction) seldom crack the way plaster does, but this does not mean that you'll never have to worry about making any repairs. The joints or seams between individual wallboard panels sometimes crack or split open because the framework of the house has settled or warped or the joints were not properly filled and taped during original construction (a combination of joint cement and perforated paper tape is used in filling joints between wallboards when they are installed). Repairs may also be required because of holes accidentally created when something heavy falls against the wallboard, or when an electrical fixture is removed.

Probably the most frequent problem that you'll run across with gypsum wallboard is nail heads popping out from the surface. When wallboards are installed the nails are recessed slightly below the surface after which joint cement is smoothed over the nail head depression to cover it. If the wrong kind or size nail has been used, or if the wall's framework settles or warps, then the nails sometimes pop back out, pushing off the compound that originally concealed them.

To cure a condition of this kind permanently, first drive the nail back in so that its head is slightly below the surface. Then drive an extra nail in a few inches above or below the old nail—only this time use a threaded or screw-type nail because these are more resistant to popping or pulling out. Use a nail with a large head and drive it in just deep enough so that your hammer makes a slight dimple in the face

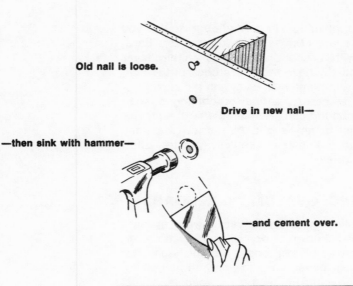

Old nail is loose.

Drive in new nail—

—then sink with hammer—

—and cement over.

Figure 35: Replacing a loose nail in wallboard.

of the wallboard, but not deep enough to tear the paper facing (see figure 35). The depression that remains is then filled in and smoothed over with ordinary spackling compound—preferably the ready-mixed paste type—using the techniques described on page 34 and 35.

If sanding is required, use only a fine grade paper and avoid sanding the paper facing on the wallboard surrounding the patch since this will only roughen it up and make the patch more obvious. One way to get a slick finish that will be perfectly smooth is to dip the putty knife into water after the spackle has had a chance to set for a minute or two. When you drag the wet blade of the knife over the surface while pressing hard you'll "glaze" the patch and make it smooth enough to leave a polished finish that will need no further treatment.

Holes that go all the way through the gypsum board so that there is no backing left are handled in the same way as a "bottomless" hole in plaster (see page 38). Another way to repair a hole of this kind—especially if it's larger than 2 or 3 inches across—is to cut the damaged piece of wallboard out completely, install a new piece as illustrated in the drawings on page 41. Use a sharp utility knife, a small utility saw, or a keyhole type saw with a pointed blade to cut the damaged piece out wide enough to expose about half of the stud (these are the vertical 2 x 4's inside the wall) on each side of the patch as illustrated in figure 36. Since studs are usually spaced 16 inches apart, center to center, the section you'll cut out will be 16 inches wide. Make it at least 8 to 10 inches high so that the piece you put in its place will be stiff enough not to buckle in the center.

Cut a new piece of gypsum wallboard (also called plasterboard) to the same size as the opening, then fasten this in place by nailing it to the studs that are partially exposed on each side. The cracks that are left at the top and bottom of the patch (between the new piece and the old surface) should be filled with joint cement and covered with perforated tape. You can also use ordinary spackling compound, but to prevent cracking it should be reinforced with a special gauze tape which many paint stores sell.

Joint cement and tape come in a combination package in most paint and hardware stores and—as illustrated in the drawings in figure 37—the application system consists of four basic steps: (1) After mixing the compound according to the directions on the package, apply it over the seam with a wide putty knife. (2) While the compound is still wet, press a length of the perforated paper tape over the seam, working it into the compound until the tape is almost fully covered with joint cement. (3) Allow the compound to dry hard, then apply a second layer of the compound only over the seam to finish the job of completely covering the tape while at the same time "feathering out" the edges of the joint so the compound blends smoothly into the face of the wallboard on each side. (4) Allow this second layer to dry hard, then apply a third layer of cement over the seam to fill in any voids or rough spots that remain and to continue the job of feathering out the edges so that the seam will be invisible. For this last application you'll need the widest putty knife you can get—preferably one that is at least 6 inches across. This will simplify the job of feathering out the seam so no ridge will be visible when the compound dries (extra-wide putty knives for this purpose are available in most paint stores—or you can use a plasterer's trowel).

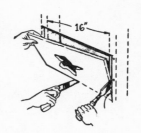

Figure 36: To repair a hole in wallboard, first cut it with a chisel along center of stud on each side of hole, then saw piece out along top and bottom.

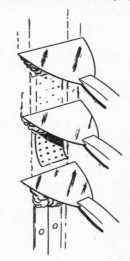

Figure 37: To hide a joint in wallboard, spread a layer of cement over it with a putty knife, as in bottom drawing; add tape and embed partially in cement (middle); trowel on final layer of cement to hide tape and to bring joint flush with wall (top).

CERAMIC TILE REPAIRS

Walls covered with ceramic tile can be considered permanent under normal conditions but occasionally a tile will pop loose because of improper installation or a structural weakness in the wall. Joints in tile walls (between the tiles or where a wall meets the floor or tub) may also need attention due to loosening or cracking out of the grout (the compound or cement that is used to fill the joints).

To replace loose tiles which have popped out, even though most of the cement or mortar is still in place, you can use any one of a number of ready-mixed tile cements which are sold in paint and hardware stores for just this purpose. They come in small cans and can be applied to the back of the tile with a small putty knife or any other convenient tool. Start by scraping off all mortar that is still stuck to the back of the tile, then brush out loose dust or crumbling material from the recess behind the tile. Next, "butter" the back of the tile with cement and press it into position so that it sits level with those on either side. Excess material that squeezes out between the joints should be scraped off immediately by using a pointed stick (a pencil with the lead point broken off works well) or a similar tool. Remember, you don't use this cement to fill the joints *between* the tiles, only to cement it in place on the wall. The joints will be filled afterward with grout (see page 43).

This same kind of cement can also be used to paste back soap dishes, paper holders, and other tile accessories that may pull loose from the wall. However, it will only work where the backing (the mortar or cement behind the tile) is still in place and relatively sound.

If you have a big hole to fill or if there is not much backing against which the fixture can be cemented, your best bet is to use a two-part epoxy cement. Epoxies are powerful adhesives that will adhere to almost anything. They come in various forms, including liquid, semi-paste, and a thick putty-like mastic. For replacing a bathroom fixture the putty-like material works best. As with all epoxies, the material comes in two parts that must be mixed together immediately before use. In the case of the putty type, there will be two differently colored compounds which you knead or blend together until a uniform color is achieved.

If the hole behind a loose soap holder or other accessory is very deep or if there is no backing at all, shove a piece of crumpled wire mesh or heavy screen wire into the opening to provide some sort of a backing for the epoxy adhesive. With this in place you can spread epoxy on the back of the fixture, as well as on the face of the mesh or mortar that remains, then push it into place until it sits in the proper position in its opening. Use strips of masking tape or pieces of string tied to something nearby to hold the fixture temporarily in place while the adhesive hardens.

Epoxy adhesives can also be used to glue back towel rod holders, glass holders, and soap dishes that break off where they project out from the wall. In this case you're better off using one of the clear liquid epoxies (they're actually amber colored). After mixing, spread the epoxy onto both halves of the broken piece, then rig up some method of taping to hold it in place until the epoxy hardens (see figure 38). Don't press or clamp it so tightly that you squeeze all of the adhesive out; use only enough pressure to hold it in the right position. Allow a minimum of 24 hours before removing the supports or applying any stress to the mended piece.

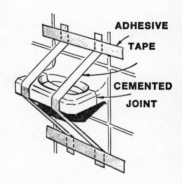

Figure 38: Repairing a broken soap dish.

Grouting Tile Walls

When you find it necessary to replace or install new grout in some of the joints on a tile wall, buy a prepared grout from your local paint or hardware store. This comes in either a powdered form which you mix with water before use or in a ready-mixed paste form. Either way, you smear it over the joint with your fingertip or with a rag wrapped around your finger. Pack it firmly into the joint, using a damp sponge or wet cloth to wipe off excess from the surface. The idea is to leave a slightly concave, neatly filled joint that will match the others in the wall.

A common problem with ceramic tile walls is a darkening or discoloring of the grouted joints. In many cases this is mildew rather than dirt so that simple scrubbing with detergent won't remove it. Try using an old toothbrush dipped into a household laundry bleach after first scrubbing with detergent. If the darkened joints are caused by mildew, the bleach will lighten them almost immediately. In extreme cases where no amount of scrubbing with bleach and detergent will do, the only other cure is to re-grout—that is, scrape out part of the old grout with a pointed tool (such as a beverage can opener) then apply fresh grout over all the joints as described above.

Another problem that pops up frequently in bathrooms that have ceramic tile on the walls is a joint that opens up around the bathtub or sink where the edge of the tile meets the top of the fixture. Since this is usually due to a slight settling of the fixtures or floor, filling the joint with fresh grout doesn't always correct the condition permanently. In a matter of weeks the joint will open up again as the fixture settles more or because of excessive vibration in the building or a structural weakness in the wall. Therefore, instead of using grout which dries hard to fill a joint of this kind, use a flexible calking material that will "give" slightly if movement occurs.

There are a number of excellent variations available for just this purpose, some made of silicone rubber and others made with an acrylic latex base. They come in tubes with a special applicator tip that enables you to squeeze out a neat ribbon just like you would toothpaste. Before you apply any of them, make sure the joint is clean and dry. The silicone rubber type is a little trickier to apply but it is generally more resistant to mildew and will last the longest. When applying, squeeze the tube steadily and keep it moving *away* from you, rather than pulling it toward you as you squeeze.

FASTENING AND HANGING THINGS ON WALLS

Unless your walls are covered with wood paneling, you can't expect to drive a nail in anywhere and have it hold when you want to hang a picture, a mirror, or a set of shelves. The walls in your house are actually hollow—that is, they are covered with plaster or gypsum board (which may vary from ⅜ to ¾ inch in thickness on each side) over a framework of 2 x 4 lumber (the 2 x 4's are called studs). The studs are supposed to be spaced 16 inches apart, center to center, but in actual practice it doesn't always work out this way—sometimes the carpenter who put up the wall was just plain careless, in other cases the width of the wall was such that the 16-inch spacing did not work out conveniently. In any case, unless building codes were violated, the studs should not be more than 16 inches apart (center to center) and after you've located one at some point in the wall you should be able to locate another either to the left or right by merely measuring 16 inches from the center of the first one.

Ideally, the easiest way to hang a heavy object on your walls would be to use long screws or nails driven into the studs. However, as a practical matter, this seldom works out since studs never seem to be located in just the spot where you want to hang that particular heavy mirror or set of shelves. To solve this problem there are a number of different kinds of specialized anchors which you can use—all designed for use in hollow walls (some can also be used in solid masonry).

Basically, these all work on the same principle: the fastener or anchor penetrates the wall surface (the plaster or gypsum board) so that it protrudes into the hollow space inside the wall. Then, depending on style, the anchor or shield splits and spreads apart (either when a long bolt in the center is tightened or when a screw or nail is driven through the middle) so that the device "expands" inside the wall cavity to grip against the back side of the wall surface as shown in the illustrations on page 46 and 47.

Broadly speaking, hollow wall fasteners can be roughly divided into three categories: metal expansion anchors, toggle bolts, and plastic anchors.

Metal expansion anchors have sleeves or shields that split apart and spread out "mushroom" style when the threaded bolt in the center is tightened. These require a hole of suitable diameter be drilled in the plaster beforehand—unless they are the drive-in type—after which the anchor (Mollys are the best known, though not the only brand) is pushed through until the flange at the head end presses tightly

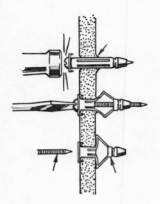

Figure 39: **Drive-in metal expansion anchor. Top: Drive it through hole. Middle and bottom: After screw is tightened it can be removed without loosing anchor.**

Figure 40: **Toggle bolt.**

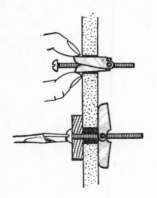

against the plaster surface. The bolt in the center is then tightened and as it turns it draws the sleeve against the back side of the wall, splitting it open and causing it to lock firmly behind the wall surface (see figure 39). The threaded bolt can then be completely unscrewed from the wall since the mushroomed anchor will remain in position. This means that you can now push the same threaded bolt through a hole in your shelf bracket, mirror bracket or other fixture and then install the fixture at your leisure (instead of having to hold it up against the wall while you drill the holes in the wall and insert the anchor).

There are also expansion type metal anchors available with their own points for driving into gypsum board. These require no hole to be drilled beforehand—all you do is hammer them home, then tighten the screw or bolt in the center to lock them in place just as you would with a conventional metal expansion anchor.

Toggle bolts have spring-actuated folding wings (see figure 40) that are hinged to a nut in the center. A long threaded bolt goes through this nut so that after a hole of the proper size is drilled in the wall, you can fold the wings and push them into the hollow space behind the plaster. The springs will then force the wings open so that as you turn the bolt the expanded wings are drawn up tight against the back side of the plaster as illustrated in figure 40. Toggle bolts of this kind will hold very heavy loads although they require a larger size hole than the expanding metal anchor type. Also you can't remove the toggle bolt once it's been tightened—if you did the wings would fall down inside the hollow wall. This means that brackets or other fixtures must be held in place and installed simultaneously with the toggle bolt (unlike anchors which you can install ahead of time).

The third type—the plastic anchor—is the quickest and cheapest to use and is more than adequate for most installations where not too much weight will be supported. This would include curtain rods, traverse rods, and shelf standards (for adjustable shelving). Plastic anchors are hollow tapered sleeves, usually made of nylon, which are designed to accept long wood screws or special threaded nails through their center.

To use these, first mark the locations on the wall where you want the anchors to go—usually by holding the shelf standard or rod bracket up on the wall and marking locations for each hole with a pencil. Then lay the shelf standard or bracket aside and drill holes of the right size for the anchors you have purchased (this should be indicated on the package), after which you push the anchor into place so that its flanged end is flush with the surface. Then, as illustrated in figure 41, the screw or nail is driven in through the hollow center. As the nail or screw penetrates, it causes the anchor to split or expand behind the plaster and against the sides of the hole so that it becomes securely anchored in the wall.

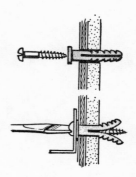

Figure 41: **Nylon anchor.**

This type is not only quicker and less expensive than a metal anchor to install, it also has a similar advantage—you need not hold the bracket or fixture in place on the wall while drilling the holes and inserting the anchors. You merely mark the location where you want the screw to go, lay the fixture (shelf bracket, mirror hanger, etc.) aside while you drill a hole in the plaster and then insert the anchor. With the anchor in place, you can hold the fixture up and drive your screw in just as you would if you were screwing into a wood surface.

For drilling holes in plaster walls, you'll need a carbide tipped bit which you can buy in any hardware store. These come in various sizes, just as ordinary drill bits do, so be sure you get the size that matches the particular anchors you'll be using. You can use a hand drill, but the job will be easier if you own (or can borrow) an electric drill. If the walls in your house are made of gypsum board (Sheetrock) then you don't need a drill—you can merely punch holes with a large nail or ice pick.

CHAPTER IV

DOOR TROUBLES

A door should close and latch smoothly—and open just as easily. When it doesn't, you not only have a nuisance, you also have a condition that will probably get worse until finally—after repeated banging, slamming, forcing, and muttering—you may be faced with the job of calling a carpenter to replace the door entirely, and maybe part of the door frame and jamb at the same time.

There is no need to let things go this far since most door problems are not especially difficult to correct—after you have located the source of trouble and learned what steps must be taken to eliminate it.

DOORS THAT STICK OR RUB

When a door sticks or rubs every time you close it, don't immediately assume that you have to attack the offending edge with a plane or heavy sandpaper. In fact, trimming should be postponed wherever possible since in many cases there are simpler and less drastic measures that will do the trick.

One of the most frequent reasons for a door sticking or rubbing along the outside edge (the edge where the lock is located) is hinge screws that have become loose, thus permitting the door to sag outward near the top, as illustrated in the drawings on page 50. Check all of the screws that hold the hinges in place to make certain that none of them have worked loose. Use a fairly large screwdriver with a blade that fits snugly in the slot of the screw to test each one and tighten any that seem loose.

If some of the screws cannot be tightened because the wood is so badly chewed up that the threads no longer grip satisfactorily, then remove the screw entirely and fill the hole with wooden toothpicks or matchsticks. Keep shoving the small sticks in, breaking each one off at the surface, until the hole is practically full of new wood (see figure 42). Then when you reinsert the screw it will have something to grab onto and can be tightened securely. If the screw is badly bent, corroded, or chewed up it should be replaced with a new one at least as large as the old one.

If none of the hinge screws are loose yet the door still sticks or rubs in one or two places along the lock edge or near the outside corners at the top or bottom of the door, then there is a good chance that either one of the hinges has not been set deep enough into the wood or one has been set too deeply (when doors are installed the hinges are recessed into the wood by cutting the wood out with a chisel). These recesses are known as mortises.

To understand how improper setting of the hinges can cause trouble, study figures 43a and b for a moment. In order for a door to open and close properly it must sit squarely inside its opening in the door frame. If it is tilted in either direction (to the left or the right when the door is fully closed) it will tend to rub in one of the corners or edges as illustrated. If the door is sticking along the bottom near the out-

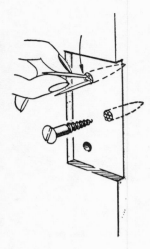

Figure 42: **Force in and break off toothpicks.**

Figure 43a; **If door rubs side of jamb near top, shim out lower hinge, or set upper hinge deeper.**

Figure 43b: **If door rubs top of jamb, shim out upper hinge, or set lower hinge deeper.**

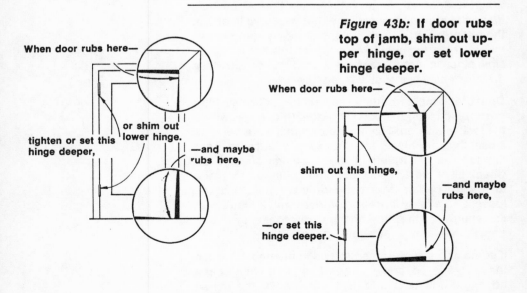

side corner (the lock edge) chances are that the lower hinge is recessed too deeply, or the top hinge is not set in deeply enough. In either case the door is tilted away from the hinges at the top so that it rubs along the bottom or along the lock edge near the top, as in figure 43a.

Assuming that there is adequate clearance around the rest of the door, the easiest way to correct a condition of this kind is to shim out the bottom hinge by placing pieces of cardboard behind the hinge leaf. You can insert cardboard shims behind the hinge leaf without removing the door from its hinges. Swing the door open about 90 degrees, then prop it in this position by wedging magazines or newspapers under it to hold it in place. Remove the screws that hold the hinge leaf to the door frame, then fold that half of the hinge out of the way and slide one or two thicknesses of cardboard (cut to the proper size) into the recess behind the hinge (see figure 44). Screw the hinge leaf back into place and try the door again. If the condition seems better but the one or two thicknesses were not enough, you may have to insert additional pieces of cardboard to effect a complete cure.

If rubbing occurs on the top edge of the door near the outside corner, you have a condition that is exactly opposite to the one just described—in other words, you need shims behind the top hinge instead of the bottom one (see figure 43b). This will tend to push the upper part of the door out from the jamb, thus pivoting the door back into a square relationship with its opening so that the upper corner swings down slightly to eliminate rubbing.

It should be obvious from a study of the drawings on page 50 that instead of shimming out one hinge, you can get the same effect by recessing the *opposite* hinge more deeply. However, this is a job that requires removing the door and doing a bit of carpentry, so attempt to solve the problem (as long as there is a little extra clearance between the door and the frame) by shimming wherever possible. If you're in doubt as to which is the cause of the problem— one hinge set too deep or the other not set deeply enough—you may be able to get a clue by swinging the door wide open and then examining the way

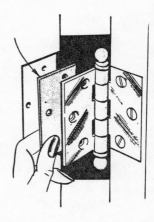

Figure 44: **Inserting a cardboard shim.**

each of the hinges has been recessed. In a proper installation both will be set equally and the face of each hinge leaf will be flush with the wood around it.

If your examination indicates that one is obviously set much deeper than the other, your best bet is to try shimming first to raise this hinge part way out of its mortise. If, on the other hand, one hinge seems to be sticking out much further than the other, you may be faced with a job that calls for removing the hinge and chiseling out the mortise more deeply (the technique for doing this is illustrated on page 54).

If the door sticks or rubs in several different places along the whole length of the lock edge, chances are that planing or sanding will be required to trim off the extra wood in the areas where rubbing occurs. If the amount of trimming required is minor, you can probably do it without taking the door down—simply prop it open with a wedge under the bottom and do the necessary planing or trimming with a small block plane held in one hand while you steady the door with your other hand. Mark the places where the door rubs and try to trim off no more than absolutely necessary to provide clearance.

If the door seems to be rubbing or sticking along most of its length, or if rubbing occurs near the lock where you cannot trim wood off without removing and then resetting the lock (quite a job even for an experienced carpenter), your best solution is to trim the door off along the hinge edge instead—but to do this you'll have to first remove the door.

To take the door off, close and latch it. Then with a hammer and a large screwdriver drive each of the hinge pins upward until you can remove them entirely, as illustrated in figure 45. Remove the bottom hinge pin first, then the top one. Next, grasp the knob and swing the door outward slowly (as though you were opening it) while gradually lifting and pulling until the hinges come apart and the door is standing on the floor. Now lay it down on its long edge so that the lock edge is down on the floor with the hinge edge facing up toward you.

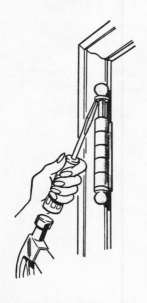

Figure 45: **Removing a hinge pin.**

To help support and steady the door in this position while you're planing the edge, there are several tricks you can use. Clamp one end to the side of a chair or table (use cardboard to protect the furniture against damage from the clamps); wedge one end into a corner of the room where two walls meet; or you can even clamp it to the side of another door (still in place on its hinges) which has been tightly wedged in the open position (see figures 46a and b). Or, a friend can hold one end while you straddle the other end as you work. In any event, you'll find it easiest to straddle the door so that you can brace it between your legs while you're planing or resetting the hinges.

Before planing the hinge side of the door, unscrew the two hinge leaves and remove them so that you'll have an unobstructed edge to work on. Then plane the door down by the amount required (this should be approximated before you take the door off, but some experimentation may still be required). In most cases you'll be able to reinstall the hinges in the same recess, but if much wood has been removed, then the hinge leaf will no longer fit flush with the surface, so you'll have to deepen the mortises by cutting them with a sharp chisel.

First tap the chisel blade vertically around the outline of the mortise, then make a series of ridge-like cuts across the width of the recess by tapping the handle lightly with a hammer so you cut part way into the wood with each blow. Finish removing the excess material by moving the chisel in from the side with a twisting, shaving action (see figure 47). The idea is to remove no more wood than necessary to reset the hinge to its original depth, so work carefully and remove small amounts of wood with each stroke. When you replace the hinge leaves, reinsert the screws in the original holes so that the hinge leaves will line up with the ones on the jamb when the door is replaced.

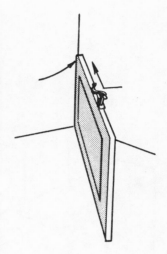

Figure 46a: **To work on the edge of a door, wedge it into a corner and plane towards the corner.**

Figure 46b: **Or, C-clamp the door to a door which is still attached to the wall and which is wedged in position.**

DOOR BINDS OR WON'T CLOSE

This is a condition where the door resists closing unless you force it (even though there is no rubbing or sticking along the edges) and tends to spring open if not latched securely. If you watch the hinges when the door is almost closed you will notice that

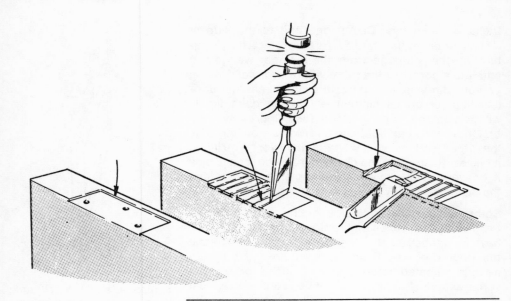

Figure 47: **If hinge mortise needs deepening (left), make a series of crosscuts with a chisel (middle), then trim out excess by working from the side (right).**

they move or bend slightly toward the door as you swing it shut the last inch or two. Nine times out of ten this is due to improper setting of one or both hinges—either they have been set too deeply in their mortises or installed so that the edge of the hinge with the hinge pin in it has been recessed deeper than the rest of the hinge.

When the whole hinge has been set too deep, the result is that the wood edge of the door meets the door frame before the hinge is fully closed—tending to force the door open. In the second case (if the hinge was improperly set so that the pin side is deeper than the rest of the leaf) the door is installed so that the hinges are fully closed before the door has swung all the way into its opening and before the lock engages.

Both of these problems can be solved by installing cardboard shims as described on page 51. In the case of hinges that have been set too deeply, install cardboard shims cut the same width and size as the hinge leaf. In the case of a hinge that has been installed with only the pin edge too deep, use narrow pieces of cardboard under the pin half of the hinge leaf only—thus tending to pivot the whole door into

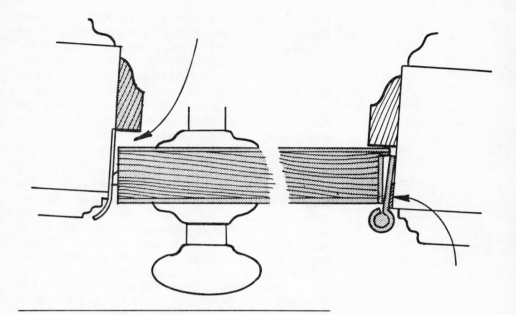

Figure 48: **If door tends to spring open, insert shim behind half of hinge leaf near hinge pin only, not behind entire leaf.**

LATCH BOLT OR LOCK DOES NOT ENGAGE

Sometimes a door will open and close easily but the latch bolt on the lock simply will not snap into the opening in the strike plate on the door frame. This is usually caused by the latch bolt not being quite in line with the strike plate opening—in most cases it's merely a matter of a fraction of an inch too high or too low. The easiest way to check this is to kneel down so that your eye is level with the lock, then close the door slowly to watch the action of the latch bolt (a flashlight usually helps). Any adjustment up or down that must be made should be handled by moving the strike plate rather than the lock.

If it's very slight you may get away with just taking the strike plate off, then filing the opening a little longer at the top or bottom as necessary. Otherwise, simply take the plate off and remount it slightly higher or lower by filling the old screw holes with wooden match sticks or toothpicks, then making new holes and relocating the plate in its new position (see figure 49). In most cases you'll have to chisel away some extra wood inside the plate's opening in order to provide clearance for the latch bolt.

Although moving the strike plate up or down slightly will usually do the trick, there will be some cases where the latch bolt will not engage the opening because the door just doesn't seem to close far enough—in other words, the door hits the stop molding (the molding against which it fits when closed) before the door closes enough for the latch bolt to slide into its opening in the strike plate. To cure this, you'll either have to move the molding out or away from the door slightly, or move the strike plate in the opposite direction (towards the door).

SLIDING DOOR PROBLEMS

Figure 49: Relocating the strike plate.

All sliding doors work on tracks and when trouble develops it's usually because one or more of the

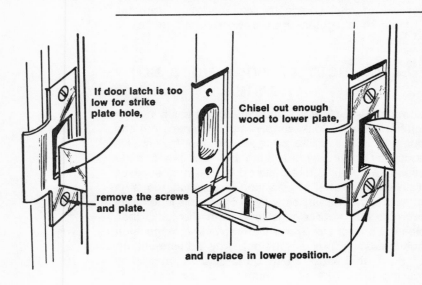

If door latch is too low for strike plate hole,

remove the screws and plate.

Chisel out enough wood to lower plate,

and replace in lower position.

doors has jumped its track. On small cabinet doors the tracks may consist simply of slotted strips of wood, metal or plastic in which the door rides (top and bottom). To permit removing the doors the top track is deeper than the bottom one so that by simply lifting up until the bottom edge of the door clears the lower track you can pull the door outward (toward you) at the bottom (see figure 50).

When doors of this kind become difficult to slide, chances are that either a slight amount of lubrication is required or some dirt has accumulated in the track to obstruct it. Use a stiff brush or a narrow nozzle on your vacuum cleaner to remove dust and dirt from these tracks at regular intervals and occasionally spray with a silicone type lubricant which leaves no stain or oily residue (don't use oil since this will attract more dirt and cake up inside the track).

Sometimes a sliding cabinet door of this kind will persist in jumping out of its bottom track every time it is moved. When this happens, check to see if there is any foreign material in the track that is interfering with its moving easily. If not, then the door may be a little too short for the height between the tracks. This may be because the doors were cut wrong to begin with, or because the top or bottom of the cabinet has warped slightly so that the tracks are now a little further apart than they were. In many cases you can cure this by removing the bottom track and putting a thin strip of cardboard or other material under it to shim it up slightly—thus bringing the tracks a bit closer together so that the doors will fit more snugly.

Larger sliding doors, such as those on closets, usually have wheels which in turn roll inside a track at the top of the frame so that the door literally hangs from this, although some older models ride with their weight resting on a track at the bottom. Since there is a wide variation in the styles of hardware used on sliding doors of this kind it is impossible to give detailed instructions for making adjustments to all of them. One of the most common types is illustrated on page 58.

Bear in mind that practically all sliding door hardware permits some adjustment or regulation of the wheeled hangers or wheeled guides on which they

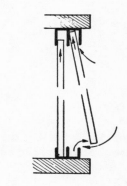

Figure 50: **To remove sliding panels, lift straight up into top channel, swing out bottom clear of its channel, and pull down.**

ride. There will usually be a screw that permits raising or lowering individual hangers to correct a condition where the door doesn't hang square or level, or to compensate for any warping of the framework (see figure 51). Doors with a track at the top usually have small guides at the bottom (fastened to the floor) to keep the door from swinging in or out, so check these to see that they have not been knocked out of alignment if the door seems to be rubbing or binding.

Sliding doors may also become stiff if the brackets that hold the wheels become bent or if they work loose where they are fastened to the door. Check the screws that hold them in place if a door starts acting up to see if they are loose and determine if the original adjustments have shifted or slipped enough to permit the door to sag out of alignment. Since the wheels are usually made of self-lubricating nylon, lubrication is almost never required but spraying with a silicone type stainless lubricant may help if there is rubbing in the bottom guides (on doors with top tracks) or stiffness in the top guides (on doors with bottom tracks).

Figure 51: **Adjusting distance between sliding door and floor.**

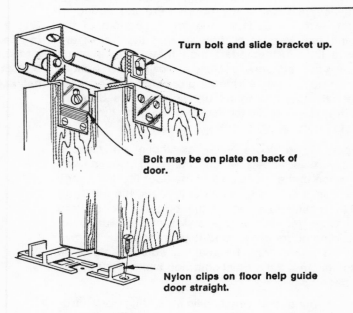

Turn bolt and slide bracket up.

Bolt may be on plate on back of door.

Nylon clips on floor help guide door straight.

LOCK PROBLEMS

Most door locks will last for a great many years if properly installed and normally require very little maintenance. Since they do have moving parts, occasional lubrication with powdered graphite will keep them from sticking and will help ensure easy opening and closing every time. Ordinary oil or grease should never be used on a lock. Instead use one of the powdered graphites or graphite-bearing oils which are designed specifically for this purpose. You can squirt this directly through the keyhole or coat the key with the lubricant, then work this back and forth inside the lock a few times to spread the graphite over the inside.

Lubricating is especially important on entrance door locks which are exposed to the weather since periodic lubrication will greatly lessen the possibility of the lock becoming frozen. If you're ever faced with the problem of opening a lock which is frozen (caused by moisture entering and freezing on the inside) the easiest way to thaw it out is to heat the key with a match or candle flame and then work this gradually into the cylinder to melt the ice on the inside. You may have to repeat the heating process two or three times but this will eventually thaw out the lock and permit the tumbler to turn. Afterward, squirt in a little penetrating type moisture-displacing lubricant to get rid of the water on the inside (this type of spray is sold in all auto supply stores for drying wet wires on automobile engines).

WEATHERSTRIPPING

In order for a door to open and close easily it has to have a certain amount of clearance or space around the edges. This creates little or no problem with most inside doors but with doors that open to the outside—or on doors that connect with unheated areas such as a garage or basement—a loose fit around the edges or along the bottom can be the cause of uncomfortable cold drafts, as well as a great deal of heat loss from the inside during the wintertime.

To eliminate these drafts and cut down on fuel waste, every door that connects with the outside—or with an unheated area such as a basement, garage, or attic which has no heat—should be sealed around the perimeter with some kind of weatherstripping. The best type is the permanent metal stripping which is normally factory installed and consists of two metal strips or channels that interlock when the door closes. If the outside doors in your house do not have this type of protection, then you have two choices—you can either call in a professional to have it installed or you can buy various types of do-it-yourself weatherstripping. These are widely available in most hardware stores and lumberyards.

Most of the do-it-yourself types are not of the interlocking, all-metal variety. They are more like gaskets (similar to the kind you have around your refrigerator door) which have a resilient or spongy facing that presses against the door when it is closed to seal out drafts and keep the heat in. The resilient facing may be made of a felt-like fabric, rubber, plastic foam, or flexible vinyl, and the weatherstripping may come in either flexible rolls or rigid strips. The flexible rolls have a flange or backing so that you can install them with tacks or small nails, while the rigid ones are made of metal or wood and look like strips of molding. You install these with either nails or small screws while the door is closed so that the flexible or cushioned part presses lightly against the inside face of the door when it is in the closed position. Nail it to the stop molding against which the door closes by working up one side, across the top, then down the other side (see figure 52).

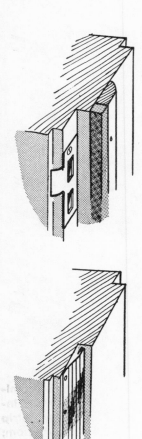

Figure 52: (Top) Wood with sponge-rubber facing; (middle) spring bronze strip nailed to jamb recess; (bottom) all rubber or plastic gasket.

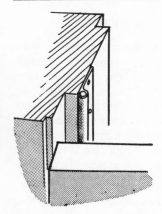

To seal drafts out at the bottom of the door there are special door bottom strips that consist of a metal molding with a flexible plastic "apron" or cushion that projects down below the edge of the door so that it brushes against the threshold or saddle when the door is closed. For a more permanent installation that will also be invisible when the door is closed, you can buy and install a special metal threshhold to replace your existing saddle (see figure 53). These metal threshholds have an insert running down the middle that consists of a flexible vinyl tube or "bubble" which projects upward so that it presses against the bottom of the door when it is closed, as illustrated in the drawing at right.

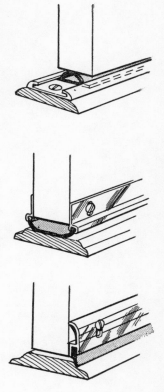

Figure 53: (Top) Aluminum channel with vinyl insert; (middle) vinyl strip fastens to door bottom; (bottom) metal-and-rubber strip is attached to the inside of door.

CHAPTER V

WINDOW REPAIRS

A window that is stuck shut, or one that won't open without a lot of unpleasant tugging and pulling, is one of those household nuisances that no one has to "live with" for long—all you need are a few tools and a knowledge of what to look for in order to cure the problem.

Residential windows come in a wide variety of sizes and styles but chances are that all the windows in your house (the ones designed to open) will fall into one of the four broad categories illustrated in figure 54—double-hung, sliding, casement, or awning.

Double-hung windows are probably the most common type and these are the kind that have two movable sashes—an upper and a lower—which slide up and down.

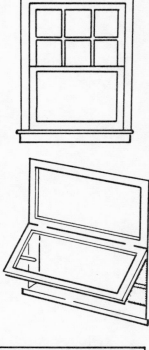

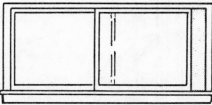

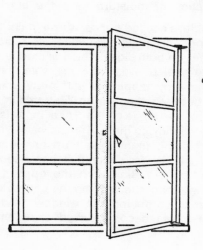

Figure 54: Window types, from top to bottom: double-hung, awning, sliding, and casement.

Sliding windows are, as the name implies, windows that slide sideways (like a sliding door) and these may have two movable (sliding) sashes or a combination of fixed and movable sashes.

Casement windows have sash frames that are hinged at one side so they swing open and close like a door. Most models have cranks or levers to simplify opening and closing (since they swing outward) and may consist of one or two movable (hinged) sashes, combined with one or two fixed sashes.

Awning windows also have hinged sash frames that swing outward but are hinged at the top instead of the sides. Since they swing out from the bottom, they look something like an awning when open—hence the name awning windows.

DOUBLE-HUNG WINDOWS

When double-hung wood windows become "frozen" or stuck shut, the trouble is usually caused by a buildup of paint around the edges of the sash frames—in other words, paint has been carelessly applied so that it forms a seal between the sash frame and the molding or window frame next to it (this can happen on the outside or on the inside). A sash can also become jammed or stuck shut because of accumulated dirt and paint in the channel or because of excessive swelling of the wood caused by absorption of moisture from the outside.

If the trouble is caused by caked-on paint (you can usually spot this if you examine the moldings and sash frames on both sides), the first step is to break or cut the seal between the movable sash and the window frame by tapping a stiff putty knife with a hammer between the two as illustrated in figure 55. As you force the blade of the knife in, twist it back and forth slightly to help pry the sash frame away from the molding, then move it up and down along the length of the frame until it has been cut free from top to bottom. Repeat on the opposite side of the window, then check along the bottom where the sash slides down behind the window sill to ensure that paint hasn't become caked along this joint as well.

Figure 55: **To loosen a stuck sash, run the blade of a putty knife between window frame and sash.**

After the sash has been loosened and raised (or lowered if it is the top sash), use a scraper or putty knife to remove excess paint from the edge of the stop molding and the inside of the window channel so as to prevent future binding. Scrape carefully to avoid chipping or gouging, using a sheet of medium grade sandpaper if necessary to smooth the molding edges and the face of the sash frame where it contacts the molding. At the same time clean any excess dirt, paint or other foreign material out of the window channel and then spray the inside of the channel with one of the various silicone lubricants (not oil) that are sold for this purpose in most hardware stores and lumberyards.

If the wood has swollen so much that no amount of lubricating or forcing will permit you to move the sash frame easily, or if you can't get at the excess paint and dirt in order to scrape it off (for example if the paint is caked on the outside of a window which you can't reach easily), then you will have to remove the stop molding on the inside by prying it off with a chisel as illustrated on page 66. Work carefully to avoid cracking the molding, letting the nails pull through the wood so that you can pull them out afterward with a claw hammer.

After this molding has been removed, the sash should slide easily since there is nothing binding against it from the inside. If it does, sand or scrape the edge of the molding that presses against the sash in order to provide added clearance before you nail it back into position. While the molding is off, scrape and clean the inner face of the sash frame as well to make certain that excess dirt or paint which has accumulated along the edges will not contribute to the problem.

If, after removing the stop molding, the lower sash still will not raise, it may be stuck with paint on the outside, or it may be binding because the wood has swollen so that the frame is too wide for the channel in which it fits. To correct this, you'll have to take the sash out of the window so that its edges can be planed or sanded to provide additional clearance. This is not as difficult as it sounds—after the stop molding has been removed the sash can be lifted out of the window quite easily (see figure 56). All

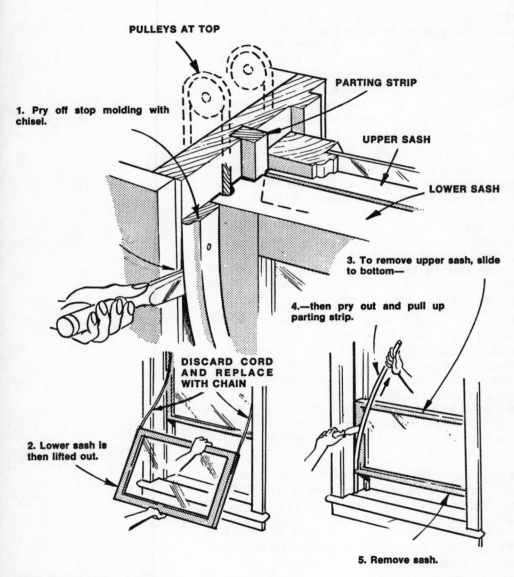

PULLEYS AT TOP

PARTING STRIP

1. Pry off stop molding with chisel.

UPPER SASH

LOWER SASH

3. To remove upper sash, slide to bottom—

4.—then pry out and pull up parting strip.

DISCARD CORD AND REPLACE WITH CHAIN

2. Lower sash is then lifted out.

5. Remove sash.

Figure 56: To remove broken cords, the sash must be removed.

you have to do is unfasten the sash cords on each side (on older windows which still use sash weights) or unscrew the mechanical spring balances that hold it in place when you raise it (see figure 57).

This, of course, applies only to the lower sash. If it becomes necessary to also remove the upper sash frame for trimming, then the parting strip (labeled in figure 56) will also have to be removed. This piece of molding separates the two window channels—one for the bottom sash and one for the top sash. It is a square wood strip that is usually pressed into a groove in the frame during original manufacture so that you can pull it out with a pair of pliers—but you'll have to be careful to avoid splitting it.

To get this strip out, lower the top sash as far as it will go, then grab the parting strip near the top of the window frame with your pliers and pull straight out while gripping firmly (on some windows there will be a couple of nails or screws that hold this strip in place, so you may have to take these out first). Before you start to pull, check for these by looking for nail heads or screw heads along the length of the strip.

As the top of the parting strip is pulled out, work your way downward pulling until the whole strip is free. In many cases the bottom rail of the upper sash frame will overlap this parting strip so that you can't pull it straight out along its full length. If so, pull the top out far enough to permit bending it so that it clears the inside of the window's frame, after which you can pull it upward to free it from its groove. The top sash can then be removed after you unfasten the sash cords or spring balances at each side. Lastly, plane or sand the edges to remove excess wood or caked-on paint, while at the same time cleaning out the window channel in which it rides.

Windows that are merely stubborn—they move, but not easily—can sometimes be cured by cleaning and lubricating the channels on each side. Use a rag and a stiff brush to clean out the dirt, then spray with a silicone lubricant or rub the inside of the channel with an old candle stub. If the window has built-in metal weatherstripping in the channels, it's often a good idea to rub this metal stripping with fine steel wool before spraying on the lubricant. The steel wool

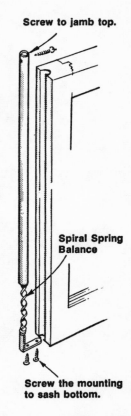

Screw to jamb top.

Spiral Spring Balance

Screw the mounting to sash bottom.

Figure 57; **Balance of a modern sash which has no cord.**

will remove dirt and pitting that may prevent the sash from sliding easily.

If the double-hung windows in your home have sash cords and weights, then make certain the cords (or chains) ride up and down easily on the pulleys that are recessed into the top of the frame on each side. Spray some graphite dust (sold for lubricating locks) into the narrow space on each side of each pulley to lubricate the shaft or use one of the aerosol type penetrating lubricants which are sold for lubricating locks and electronic mechanisms (available in most auto accessory stores).

When a double-hung window doesn't work properly because the sash cord is broken on either side, the best cure is to replace the cord with chain after first removing the sash from the window frame as described on page 66 and 67. After the bottom sash is out and the cords disconnected, there should be an access panel or cut-out visible in the wood channel on either side. This panel is provided so that you can gain access to the sash weights that hang in the hollow space behind the frame. The panel is held in place with one or two screws that will have to be removed first. If it has never been removed from the window before, it's possible that you won't be able to see it because its outline will be completely hidden by caked-on paint. If so, you may have to scrape some of the paint away from the back of the window channel to find the cover, or try tapping with a hammer until cracks appear around the edge to outline the removable cover.

Once you've found the pocket cover and removed the screws that hold it in place, pry it out with a chisel or stiff putty knife so that you can reach inside to get at the sash weights. On some older houses this cover may never have been cut out completely when the window was originally assembled. If this is the case, you will have to use a keyhole saw to finish the cut so that the cover can be removed. After the sash weight has been lifted out with its broken cord attached, feed new chain through the pulley at the top so that it drops down low enough for you to reach through the pocket cover opening and grab it (see figure 58).

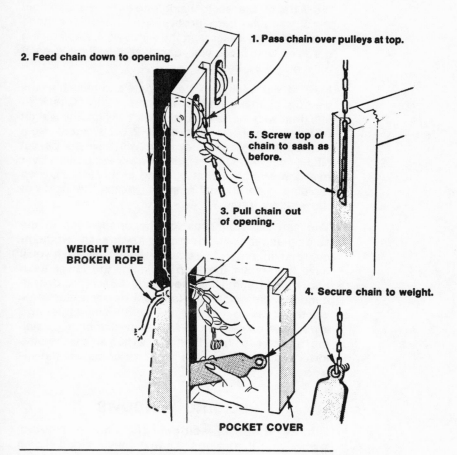

2. Feed chain down to opening.

1. Pass chain over pulleys at top.

5. Screw top of chain to sash as before.

3. Pull chain out of opening.

WEIGHT WITH BROKEN ROPE

4. Secure chain to weight.

POCKET COVER

If you have trouble feeding the chain down, try tying a large washer to the end to add weight. Attach the end of the chain inside the weight box to the top of the old sash weight, using the special hooks or clips provided. To determine the length of chain you will need for each side, you can use the old length of broken cord as a guide, or you can set the sash temporarily in place in the window frame while you measure the amount of chain needed to go up through the pulley and down inside to the weight.

After you've attached the chain to the weight, put the weight back inside its pocket in the window

Figure 58: **Replacing a broken sash cord.**

frame, then fasten the outside end of the chain to the side of the sash, using one or two nails to hold the chain in the cord groove. This should be done with the sash resting on the windowsill. Replace the cords on both sides with chain at this time even if only one was broken.

Now fit the sash into its channel and raise it all the way up to make certain it works freely. Check to see that with the sash as high as it will go, the weight on the inside still hangs at least 2 or 3 inches from the bottom—if not, the chain will have to be cut slightly shorter. Then replace the access panel cover over the weight pocket opening and renail the stop molding in its original position against the inside of the window frame.

You can replace cords for the upper sash in the same manner as you do for the lower sash. Remember that in order to remove the upper sash you'll have to remove the stop molding, the lower sash and the parting strip (see page 66). Also, bear in mind that the weight pocket cover on each side provides access to the weights for both the upper and lower sash on each side. When reassembling, install the upper sash first, then the parting strips, then the lower sash and finally the stop moldings on the inside.

SLIDING WINDOWS

Sliding windows seldom give much trouble, particularly if they are made of metal. Wood sliding windows will sometimes get stuck because of dried paint which has caked on around the edges—either on the inside or the outside. To free up a window of this kind, pry with a stiff putty knife and a hammer similar to the method illustrated on page 64. Then when the window has been opened, scrape paint away from the edges and use sandpaper to smooth off the face of the frame.

All sliding windows should have their tracks lubricated regularly to keep them working smoothly, so if yours are hard to move the trouble can most likely be cured by cleaning and lubricating the tracks. Use a stiff brush to remove the dirt and rub with medium grade steel wool if the track seems pitted, corroded or caked with accumulations of any kind. The safest and most effective lubricant to use is an aerosol type silicone spray which lubricates without leaving a sticky residue (oil attracts dirt and may attack the plastic rollers on some windows).

CASEMENT WINDOWS

Casement windows which hinge at the sides may be made of wood or metal but when trouble develops it is most often due to difficulty with the levers or crank mechanism used to open and close the windows. On wood windows this will usually consist of a simple sliding rod connected by two pivots, one on the window sill and one on the inside face of the sash frame. If the rod doesn't slide in and out easily, try lubricating it and the fittings through which it slides, as well as the two pivoting pieces to make sure they turn easily. Lightweight lubricating oil or a penetrating type aerosol lubricant can be used for this. If the rod that pushes the window open seems to bind at some point, take it off and roll it on a flat surface to see if it's bent or to see if there are any sharp nicks that cause it to bind in the piece of hardware through which it slides.

Metal casement windows may also have a simple sliding rod to push them open or pull them closed but in most cases there is a crank that turns a gear which in turn swings a long lever in or out to open or close the window. In come cases this mechanism may become stiff or inoperative because of lack of lubrication, while in others the mechanism may have been caked with dirt and hardened lubricant so that it no longer works easily. Either way, if the crank or handle doesn't work smoothly, your best bet is to first try working some oil into the mechanism by dripping it into the joint where the handle meets the case or by reaching through the outside and squirting it in through the slot in the frame where the actuating lever comes out.

If this doesn't free it up, then it's possible that the gears on the inside are worn so badly that they no longer mesh properly and the entire assembly will have to be taken apart and cleaned out. This involves removing the handle, (there's a small set screw that holds it in place) and taking out the two bolts that hold the case in place against the window frame. The actuating lever on the outside is attached to the gear works so it has to come off with the case, meaning that you must detach it from the back of the hinged sash frame. Usually this means sliding it along the slot in which it fits until it comes out, but in some cases it may mean unscrewing a hinged fitting which secures the end of the arm to the sash frame.

Once the unit has been completely removed, you can flush out the inside with kerosene to remove dirt and hardened lubricant, then apply fresh grease to the inside (a white nonstaining type is easiest to use). If the handle turns easily but the gears on the inside do not mesh properly or if they have so much play that they don't work smoothly, then you may have to replace the unit entirely. Building materials dealers and lumberyards who sell casement windows can order a replacement, but take the old one with you to be certain you get one that matches exactly.

Since all casement windows have hinges, stiffness can also be caused by hinges that get rusty or become caked with dirt or are in need of lubrication. It's a good idea to put a drop or two of lightweight machine oil on each hinge at least once a year and to scrape off rust and touch up with paint as soon as rusty spots are noticed (see figure 59).

Figure 59: **Oiling casement hinge.**

Sometimes casement windows cause problems because they will not lock completely or shut tightly. Metal casements have a hook-type locking handle that reaches through a slot in the frame to engage the edge of the sash when it is fully closed. If this hook does not pull the sash tight enough against the frame, you may be able to get a snugger fit by removing the locking handle from the window (it's held in place by two screws) then placing a thin shim of cardboard or sheet plastic behind it (as illustrated in figure 60) before you reinstall it with the two screws. This shim will tend to draw the hinged sash inward by shortening the amount which the hook protrudes on the outside so that it will pull the sash more tightly against the frame when the handle is pressed all the way down.

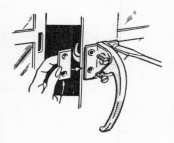

Figure 60: **Cardboard under handle base tightens grip of handle when shut.**

WEATHERSTRIPPING

Loose fitting windows not only rattle noisily, they also allow cold drafts to enter and can result in a great deal of wasted heat—thus raising fuel bills much higher than necessary. To prevent this, good construction calls for weatherstripping to be installed on all windows to seal the edges and prevent leaks around the movable sash. Ideally, this should be installed during initial construction when a permanent metal type can be recessed into the edge of the sash and the frame, but if you live in an old house or apartment that does not have this built-in protection there are ways to deal with cold drafts and wasted heat.

As described on page 59 and 60 (Chapter IV, DOORS) there are a wide variety of weather stripping materials available in hardware stores and lumberyards that are specifically designed for do-it-yourself installations. Most of those described for use on doors can also be used on double-hung windows—this includes the rigid metal or wood moldings with resilient facings made of felt, rubber, plastic foam, or flexible vinyl. You nail these to the inside stop molding so that the flexible face presses against the sash—but do not nail them so snug against the sash that it becomes hard to move the sash up or down. While any of these can be used around a lower sash, you may have trouble installing them around the upper sash on a double-hung window since these strips are often too wide to fit on top of the parting strip between the two sashes when the lower sash is raised—but they can be installed on the outside.

Flexible weatherstripping which you can buy in rolls or coils will probably be easiest for you to install and is most adaptable for use around windows. The principle is basically the same for all: a resilient material on the edge presses against the face of the window with enough pressure to seal out leaks without appreciably affecting your ability to slide the sash up and down. Some are installed with small nails (usually supplied with each roll of weatherstripping) while others come with an adhesive backing so that they will adhere when pressed into position. To seal off windows that will seldom if ever be opened, you can buy a string-like putty or caulking material that can be pressed into place with your fingers (it works something like modeling clay). It never really dries, so whenever you wish you can merely pull it out and even reuse it later on. This same material is also ideal for sealing leaks or openings around window-mounted air conditioning units in the summer.

To seal casement windows that do not have factory-installed weatherstripping, the easiest material to use is an adhesive-backed plastic or rubber foam which you can buy in rolls and merely press into place around the edge of the window frame so that the sash will press against it when closed—the foam rubber or plastic acts as a gasket to help seal the openings around the edges of the sash frame. Several companies also make special U-shaped plastic channel strips which slip over the edge of metal casement windows to form a resilient gasket around the sash so that an airtight seal will be formed when you close it tightly.

REPLACING A BROKEN PANE OF GLASS

A broken pane of glass is not particularly difficult to replace yourself—in many cases doing the job yourself is easier than trying to find someone who will come promptly when you want them to. You can replace the glass without removing the sash, providing you can get at the window easily from the outside. If the window is on the second floor or where climbing to the outside might be difficult, your best bet is to remove the sash completely (see page 66) so you can work on it from inside.

The first thing you will have to do is remove all of the old, broken glass by pulling the pieces out gently. To avoid cutting your hands wear heavy work gloves or use several thick rags to grab hold of the glass slivers. In most cases the pieces will pull out easily but if you run across a stubborn section rock it back and forth gently to break the bond between the glass and the putty, then pull it straight out to remove it (see figure 61).

The next step is to remove all of the old, hardened putty by scraping it out with a small chisel or large screwdriver. If the putty is extra stubborn, you may have to tap the chisel with a hammer but work carefully to avoid gouging the molding in which the glass fits. Use a stiff brush or piece of steel wool to clean the wood thoroughly, then paint the rabbet (recess) with a coat of linseed oil or a light coat of thinned-down house paint. This coating is important to seal the wood so that when you apply fresh putty the pores will not draw all the oils out of the compound and thus leave it brittle.

Measure the opening in which the glass must fit, then have your hardware dealer cut you a new pane the right size. When measuring, remember that the piece of glass should be approximately ⅛ inch less in width and height than the actual opening in order to allow for a small amount of clearance on all sides. Before pressing the new piece of glass into place, apply a thin layer of glazing compound to the inside of the recess around all sides (see figure 61). This "bed" of glazing material is necessary to ensure a water-tight seal after the glass is in place, as well as to cushion the glass and correct for irregularities in the frame. Although you can use either glazing compound or linseed oil putty, you'll find glazing compound a lot easier to work with—and it will not get as brittle as putty.

Press the glass firmly against the bed of glazing compound so it seats smoothly around all edges, then fasten it permanently in position by inserting glazier's points around the side. Glazier's points are small triangular shaped bits of metal which you can buy where you get the glass, and small panes will usually require four to hold them properly—two on each vertical side. Larger pieces should have three or more equally spaced along each side, as well as at least one at the top and bottom (a rule of thumb is one glazier's point every 6 or 7 inches along each side).

Remember it is these glazier's points that are supposed to hold the glass in place, not the glazing compound, so don't leave them out. They're not hard to install, you just push them in with the end of a

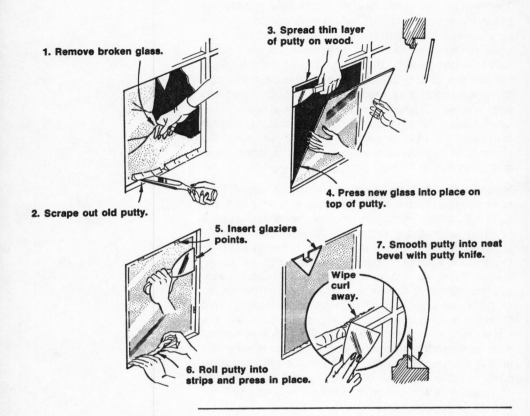

1. Remove broken glass.

2. Scrape out old putty.

3. Spread thin layer of putty on wood.

4. Press new glass into place on top of putty.

5. Insert glaziers points.

Wipe curl away.

7. Smooth putty into neat bevel with putty knife.

6. Roll putty into strips and press in place.

Figure 61: **Replacing a broken pane.**

putty knife or a screwdriver as shown in the drawing above. Some brands also have little flanges or bent-up edges which make it easier to push them into place without slipping.

With the glass secured, you're ready to finish off with glazing compound around the outside. The easiest way is to first roll the material into strips a little thinner than a pencil, then lay these into the recess around the edge of the sash, pressing it in place with your fingers. Now use your putty knife to smooth it into a neat bevel that runs from the edge of the sash molding up onto the glass as shown. Properly done, this should form a triangular shaped bead that will be flush with the outer edge of the molding on the outside and will come high enough up on the glass to match the level of the wood molding on the inside. The main thing is to make certain that you pack the compound down firmly and leave no cracks or open seams into which water can seep.

The technique for glazing metal sash frames is similar to that of wood frames, except that instead of glazier's points there will be special spring clips that hold the pane of glass in place. Otherwise, you use the same glazing compound (never linseed oil putty on metal sash) and "bed" the glass down with a layer of the glazing compound just as you would for wood sash.

Some metal windows don't use putty at all—the glass is held with a rubber strip of molding, which is in turn held in place by screws. Re-glazing this type of window is simple—you simply unscrew the rubber seal, remove the broken glass, then re-install the seal on top of the new glass, other metal windows have the glass held in place with a plastic or rubber gasket that requires a special tool to remove and reinstall it. With this type of glazing system (often used on storm sash and storm doors) you may have to call in a professional to do the job.

REPAIRING WINDOW SCREENS

Repairs to window screens actually fall into two categories—repairs to the screen frame and repairs to the screen wire or mesh. If the frames are made of metal, then chances are that they'll never need fixing—if they get badly bent or cracked then complete replacement is the only cure. Window screens with wood frames sometimes do get loose or wobbly and can be easily repaired by screwing metal corner irons or corner plates onto the corners to reinforce the joints. Hammer the frame tightly together to close the joint before you install the reinforcing irons and be sure you use brass or galvanized metal pieces to avoid rust stains later on.

Repairs to the screen wire are feasible as long as the tear or hole is not too big. If the screen is covered with metal wire then you can patch the hole with small, ready-made screen patches which you can buy in most local hardware stores. Or you can use a scrap piece of matching wire mesh that you may have had left over. The patch should be larger than the damaged area and should have a few wires

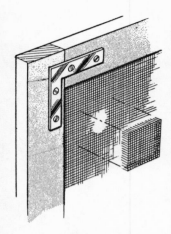

Figure 62: **Patching hole in screen. Note L-bracket in corner to reinforce weak joint.**

unraveled around the edges so that there is about a half-inch of each wire exposed. On ready-made patches these pieces of wire will be bent at right angles to the surface as illustrated in figure 62, but if you're making your own patch you'll have to bend the wires yourself. First push the piece on over the hole so that the bent pieces of individual wire go through the mesh and stick out on the other side. Then, by folding these over tightly on the back you'll lock the patch firmly in place.

This type of patch won't work on plastic or fiberglass mesh, so if you have this kind of screening on your windows there are two other techniques you can use. If the hole is small, just cover it with a few dabs of clear nail polish or clear household cement, building it up in layers if necessary until the entire tear or hole is filled in. If the hole is too big for this, cut a piece of scrap mesh with scissors and cement it in place with clear household cement. For any of these patching methods to look reasonably neat, you should make every effort to line up the strands or wires on the patch so that they match the pattern on the existing mesh.

Installing New Wire

If the screen wire is so badly torn that replacement is the only cure, your best bet is to buy new mesh made of fiberglass or plastic. This type is much easier to stretch and cut than metal mesh and you'll never have to worry about it corroding or causing stains on the walls of your house—it will never need painting or varnishing.

When measuring for the amount you will need, remember to buy material that is at least 6 or 8 inches wider and longer than the screen frame to allow for enough excess to permit you to stretch and hold the material more easily. The excess can be cut off with scissors later.

On wooden screen frames, start by prying off the old moldings with a screwdriver or putty knife, working carefully to avoid cracking them (don't worry if one piece splits—you can always buy a new length at the lumber yard). After the moldings are off, rip off the old screen wire and pull out any tacks or staples that are left. Then, with the screen frame lying flat, fold over a ½-inch "hem" at one end of the plastic mesh and staple this into place across one end of the screen frame, driving staples through the double thickness to ensure a firmer grip. If you don't have a staple gun you can probably rent one from your local hardware store or lumberyard or you can use rustproof copper tacks—but stapling is faster and a lot easier.

To minimize the possibility of wrinkles and to simplify stretching the plastic mesh smoothly, start stapling across the top or bottom by driving the first staple into the center and work out toward the corner in each direction. After you have one end stapled in this manner, stretch the mesh by hand as tight as you can to the other end, then drive your first staple in the center again. Now you can smooth it out by working from the center toward each of the corners, alternating staples so you drive one first to the right side of the center staple, then to the left side, then back to the right again and so on.

After both ends have been stapled, you can stretch the mesh sideways and start stapling each of the long sides—again starting from the center and working out toward the corners (see figure 63). Since in all of these stretching and stapling operations you'll need excess material to give you a hand grip for pulling and holding while you staple, the simplest method is to leave the mesh wider and longer than necessary and use the excess to provide a grip while you're working. After the wire has been stapled down around all four sides, a sharp knife and a straightedge can be used to trim off the excess (some people prefer to nail the moldings back first then trim off the excess afterward). When replacing the wood moldings, use rustproof brads if possible and touch up bare spots or new pieces with paint to protect the wood.

On metal screen frames the plastic wire mesh is held in place by a metal or plastic spline or strip that fits into a groove around the edge of the screen frame as illustrated in figure 64. As you can see, this wedges the plastic wire in place so no tacks or staples are needed. To replace screening on this type of frame, pry out the plastic spline first, using a screwdriver or dull putty knife. Then pull out the

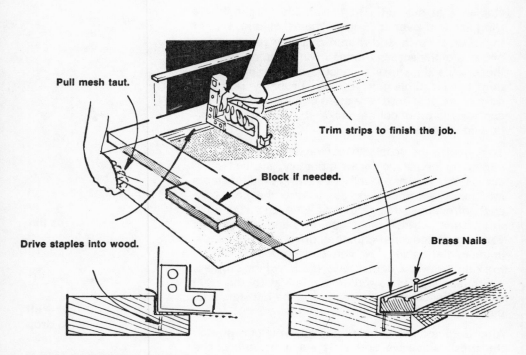

Pull mesh taut.

Trim strips to finish the job.

Block if needed.

Drive staples into wood.

Brass Nails

Figure 63: **installing new screen wire.**

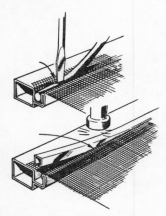

Figure 64: **(Top) Neoprene strip is forced into groove with screwdriver; (bottom) aluminum strip is hammered into slot.**

old screen wire and cut a new piece of screen mesh an inch or two bigger around all edges. Lay this piece in place on top of the metal screen frame, then trim off the corners of the mesh at a 45-degree angle, using a sharp knife and making this cut in such a way that it comes right across the corner of the groove in which the spline fits. The reason for trimming the material in this manner is to avoid the bunching up that would otherwise occur in each corner.

With the piece of mesh still in place on top of the frame (and the corners trimmed off) lay the spline for one of the long sides on top of the screening so that it is directly over the groove into which it fits. Then use a large screwdriver or a scrap piece of ⅛-inch thick hardboard or wood to tap the spline back into its groove, beginning at one end and working your way down along its entire length (see figure 64). As you force the spline back into the groove, it will press the screen mesh in with it, thus locking it securely in place.

After you've installed the spline along one side of the frame, repeat the process on the other side, only this time pull the mesh tight with one hand as you go—by grabbing the excess material on the *outside* of the spline. Then replace the spline on each of the short sides, after which you can use a sharp knife or razor blade to trim off the excess on all four sides.

WINDOW SHADE REPAIRS

Window shade rollers have a flat metal pin at one end that is attached to a spring on the inside of the roller. This flat pin fits into a vertical slot in one of the window shade brackets so that as you pull the shade down (unrolling it) the pin cannot turn (see figure 65). Since this pin is connected to a spring inside the roller, with the other end of the spring secured inside the roller, the result is that as the shade is pulled down it winds up the spring.

Figure 65: **Pawl keeps flat pin from unwinding.**

The reason the spring does not immediately unwind (and thus let the shade fly back up to its original position) when you let go of it is that there is a small pawl-and-ratchet mechanism on the outside that catches and holds the roller in place when you let it go (see figure 66). When you're ready to raise the shade you give it a slight downward pull and this causes the pawl to flip up out of its locked position so that the wound-up spring on the inside lets go and pulls the shade back up. The other end of the shade roller merely has a round pin which fits into a hole in the bracket to act as a pivot which supports the opposite end of the shade.

Figure 66: **(Top) Pull shade down a bit to drop pawl; (middle) rapid raising keeps pawl loose; (bottom) stopping lets pawl fall back to lock. Note flat pin in center is always vertical.**

When a shade keeps unwinding by itself or doesn't have enough tension to rewind itself after you've pulled it down, the trouble is caused by not enough tension in the spring inside the roller.

The cure for this is simple, as shown in figure 67: (1) Pull the shade down as far as it will go. (2) With the shade fully unrolled, lift the roller out of its brackets and then with your hands roll the fabric up around the roller as indicated in the drawing. (3) Place the rolled-up shade back in the brackets then

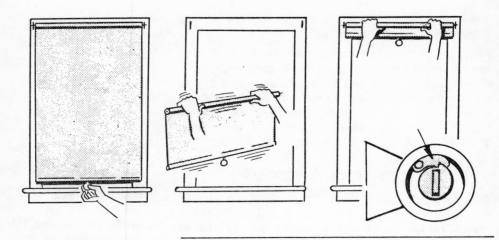

Figure 67: Remedying a sluggish shade. (Left) Pull shade all the way down; (middle) lift roller out of brackets and roll shade up by hand; (right) replace roller in brackets with pawl on top.

pull it down slowly to see how the tension feels. If it's still too weak, pull it halfway down then repeat the process of lifting the shade out of the brackets and rolling it up by hand. (4) Try the shade again and, if necessary, repeat the whole process once more.

If the trouble is just the opposite—the spring is wound up too tight and has so much tension that it literally flies out of your hand every time you try to raise it, reverse the process as follows: (1) Raise the shade all the way up to the top. (2) Lift the rolled-up shade out of the brackets, then unroll it by hand to about half its length. (3) Replace the roller in its brackets and check the tension on the shade. If it's still too tight repeat the process once more.

Sometimes a window shade will have the proper tension in its spring but it will refuse to catch or stay put after you've pulled it down to the desired position. This kind of problem is caused by the fact that the pawl-and-ratchet mechanism is not engaging properly. Sometimes dirt keeps the pawl from dropping into the ratchet on the pin, while in other cases it sticks and fails to drop into place when it should. You may be able to correct this condition by removing the shade from its brackets and then cleaning out the space around the flat pin (where the pawl-and-ratchet mechanism is located) with a small stiff artist's brush or an old toothbrush. Blow out any dirt or lint that you see, then spray a little powdered graphite over the mechanism to free it up. If this doesn't work then you'll have to buy a new shade roller. They're available in all shade stores and are quite inexpensive (for average size windows they will cost only a dollar or two).

To change rollers, first pull out the staples which hold the shade to the old roller, then restaple the fabric on the new roller. One word of caution—when stapling the fabric onto the new roller be sure you get it on straight by matching the edge of the fabric with the inked line on the wood roller. If the fabric is not perfectly straight, the shade will roll off at an angle and will not operate smoothly. If you don't have a staple gun you can use carpet tacks, but stapling is faster and easier (many stores will rent you a staple gun if you don't own one).

Sometimes a window shade will stick or not roll up properly even though there is nothing actually wrong with it—the trouble is in the brackets supporting the shade, rather than in the shade itself. Check to see if the brackets are bent or caked with paint, or if they are loose (due to loose nails or screws). Since these brackets cost only a few cents apiece, it is always best to replace them if they look doubtful. Pay particular attention to the slotted bracket (the one that holds the flat pin). When this gets worn it won't hold the flat pin (on the end of the roller) vertical—if the pin tends to turn slightly it may slip and let the spring on the inside unwind or it may keep the ratchet mechanism from engaging properly when you pull the shade down (see figure 68).

If there is too much clearance between the brackets, i.e., if the roller seems too short so that the shade always keeps falling out—then either your shade roller is too short or the brackets have been improperly mounted in the first place. If the difference is slight (say ¼ inch or less) then you can correct the trouble by taking the shade off and pulling the round pin out slightly with a pair of pliers so that it projects out a bit more. You can also bend the bracket slightly or shim it out by putting a thin piece of wood or heavy cardboard behind it.

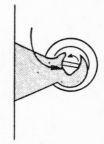

Figure 68: Worn bracket allows rollers to spin.

If the brackets seem too close together so that the shade binds or rubs against them when it's unrolled, then the opposite condition is causing the problem, i.e., the shade roller is a bit too long or the brackets have been mounted too close together. The cure here is to either cut the roller slightly shorter (you do this by pulling out the round pin, prying off the metal cap under it, then sawing the needed amount off the end of the wood roller), or by bending or hammering the brackets outward slightly to provide a little extra clearance between them.

VENETIAN BLIND REPAIRS

There are essentially only two problems which are likely to occur with venetian blinds: either the ladder tapes that support and tilt the slats tear, or the cord which actuates the tilting or raising mechanism becomes frayed and torn. You can take care of both of these problems at home since replacement cords and prefabricated replacement ladder tapes are widely available in hardware, houseware, and department stores in most communities.

As illustrated in figure 69, venetian blinds—regardless of whether they have wooden or metal slats—are quite similar in construction and operation. The individual slats rest on horizontal strips of narrow cloth tape which are sewed to the two wider vertical strips that complete the "ladder" on each side. These tapes are fastened to the wood bar (on wood blinds) or the metal channel (on metal blinds) at the top and to the underside of the bottom bar at the lower end of the blind. On wood blinds the tape is stapled to the bottom of the wood bar; on metal blinds the tape is held in place by a spring clamp that fits over the metal bar.

To replace the tapes on the blind, lower it all the way down and unfasten the tapes from the bottom rail by pulling out the staples or prying off the clamp. Next, untie the knots at the ends of the lift cord which raise the blind (there will be one at each end of the bottom rail) so that you can pull the cords out through the top of the blind to free up all the slats. Then slide all the slats out sideways so that only the two ladder tapes are left hanging down at each end. To remove these tapes, unfasten them from the top, then attach the new tapes in the same way (on wood blinds the tapes will be stapled to the tilt mech-

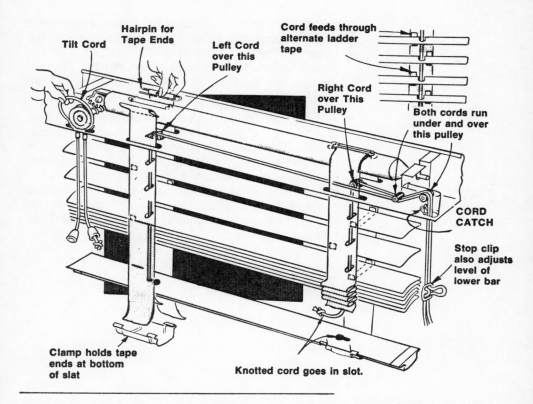

Tilt Cord

Hairpin for
Tape Ends

Left Cord
over this
Pulley

Cord feeds through
alternate ladder
tape

Right Cord
over This
Pulley

Both cords run
under and over
this pulley

**CORD
CATCH**

Stop clip
also adjusts
level of
lower bar

Clamp holds tape
ends at bottom
of slat

Knotted cord goes in slot.

anism at the top; on metal blinds they will probably be held in place by special clips).

Replace all of the slats by positioning them across the individual ladder strips, then thread the cords back through them, being careful that the cord runs down through the center so that alternate ladder strips are on opposite sides of the cord as they were originally. Pull the end of the cord through the bottom bar and retie the original knot to put the blind back in operating position.

If the lift cord is broken or frayed then you can replace it with a new one at the same time. Starting at the bottom left, thread the new cord up through the hole in the bottom bar, then up through the hole in each slat. Next, run it across the top and down through the lift cord lock-and-pulley mechanism as shown. Extend it down until it makes a loop approximately as long as the original cord, then run it back up over the second pulley and down through

Figure 69. **Typical metal venetian blind.**

the slats on the right hand side. Finish by bringing it out through the hole in the right hand end of the bottom bar and tie a new knot after cutting it to the proper length. Then restaple or reclamp the lift tapes to cover the knots in the underside of the bottom rail.

All venetian blinds have a second cord which operates the tilt mechanism to open or close the blinds. This cord simply loops over a pulley driving a worm gear that actuates the tilt tube to which the ladder tapes are attached. If this cord needs replacing, cut a new piece the same length as the old one. Thread this over the pulley (after removing the old cord) and attach the plastic or metal tassels at each end when finished.

CHAPTER VI

ELECTRICAL REPAIRS

It has been said that all electrical repairs can be divided into two categories—those you can safely tackle yourself and those that should only be performed by a licensed electrician. There is no definite division into which category each type of household electrical repair falls since this will depend on your own experience and ability. Even if you've done nothing more than change a light bulb, the contents of this chapter will describe many minor and frequently encountered electrical problems that you can safely correct yourself—if you follow directions and observe a few common sense precautions such as insuring that power has been safely shut off by removing the appropriate fuse or turning off the circuit breaker.

FUSES AND CIRCUIT BREAKERS

In every home or apartment electric power comes in through a main service panel (service entrance) which is part of or next to the fuse box. The current is divided into a series of separate circuits to supply power to various lights, appliances and electrical outlets throughout the house. Each of these individual circuits is protected by its own fuse or circuit breaker and there is another, much larger fuse or circuit breaker (there may be more than one) that protects the entire service panel—through which all power to the individual circuits flows. Fuses and circuit breakers are actually the weakest links in the electrical system since they act as built-in "safety valves" for each circuit (or, in the case of the main fuse, for the entire system). If a short circuit or dangerous overload occurs in any part of the house the fuse will blow (or the circuit breaker will open) before the wires in that circuit can get hot enough to melt or start a fire. The idea is to keep current flow from exceeding the safe capacity of the wires, while at the same time providing a central point where you can exercise control.

In a private home the fuse box is usually located somewhere in the basement next to, or as part of, the main service entrance and the main switch that controls all power to the house. In most apartments there is a small fuse box located in or near the entrance hall, though in some older apartment houses the fuse boxes for all apartments may be located in the basement of the building.

It is important that you know where the fuse box is and that each of the fuses are labeled so that you know what circuit it controls. If this hasn't already been done, you should do it at the first opportunity. The easiest way is to unscrew one fuse at a time while all lights in the house are turned on and then go around to see which lights and appliances are affected. At the same time, carry a plug-in of some kind so that you can check each of the wall outlets to see which has no power when that particular fuse is removed. Then make a list of the rooms or receptacles controlled and post this conspicuously on or near the fuse box. Repeat this for each fuse (or circuit breaker) to obtain a complete list of what is included in each branch circuit so that when and if trouble does develop you'll immediately know which fuse has to be removed. Remember that certain large appliances such as refrigerators or washing machines should be on their own circuit so that if your house is properly wired some fuses will actually control only the one major appliance.

The fuses normally used in home lighting circuits are of the screw-in type as pictured in figure 70. These have transparent plastic windows at the top so that you can see when one is blown—either this window will turn black or you will be able to see that the metal strip on the inside is broken (melted by the excessive current flow).

Heavier duty circuits, such as those which supply power to a kitchen stove, hot water heater or clothes dryer usually have cartridge-type fuses instead of screw-in or plug type fuses. The smaller ones (those rated below 60 amperes) have a plain metal cap at

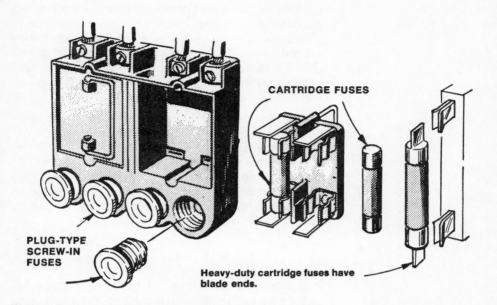

CARTRIDGE FUSES

PLUG-TYPE
SCREW-IN
FUSES

Heavy-duty cartridge fuses have
blade ends.

Figure 70: **Fuse types.**

each end which snaps into spring metal clips in the box. Larger ones (above 60 amperes) have flat metal blades at each end as illustrated.

When a fuse "blows" it has to be replaced (after the cause of the trouble has been determined), so keep spares on hand of the same capacity as the ones in your fuse box. The capacity is stamped on top, so check carefully before replacing one. *NEVER* replace a fuse with one of a larger rated capacity since this is a dangerous practice that eliminates the safety factor which a fuse is designed to provide. For example, most common household circuits have 15-ampere fuses because this is the maximum safe current which the wires in that circuit can carry; replacing the 15-ampere fuse with a 20-ampere fuse would permit the wires to carry more current than they are designed to handle—which could result in dangerous overheating and might cause a fire or breakdown of the wiring inside the walls.

CIRCUIT BREAKERS

Circuit breakers differ from fuses in that they are permanently installed switches with thermostatic controls which cause them to switch off when an overload occurs (the overload causes overheating). They seldom, if ever, have to be replaced—when they are thrown to the "off" position by a short circuit or overload you can throw them back to the "on" position by simply flicking the toggle and thus resetting (after the trouble has been corrected).

The advantages of this kind of installation are obvious—you eliminate worrying about having replacement fuses on hand and can spot the trouble instantly since the breaker's handle moves to the "off" position when a short occurs in that circuit (see figure 71). In addition, circuit breakers prevent anyone from accidentally (or purposely) inserting the wrong size fuse in its place.

WHEN A FUSE BLOWS

If a household fuse blows or a branch circuit breaker clicks off shortly after you're plugged in an appliance or lamp, then the trouble is either caused by a defect in that appliance or by the fact that the circuit is overloaded (appliances and lamps totaling too high a wattage are plugged in at one time). Either way, the first thing to do is unplug all portable lamps and appliances on that circuit, then replace the fuse or switch the circuit breaker back on. If it blows again immediately before plugging anything back in, the

Figure 71: **Circuit-breaker box.**

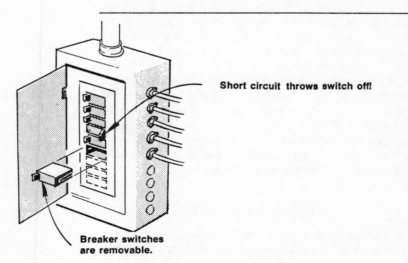

Short circuit throws switch off!

Breaker switches
are removable.

trouble is in the internal wiring or in one of the permanently wired fixtures and this is a job for a professional electrician to locate and repair.

In most cases, the fuse or circuit breaker should stay on, indicating that the trouble is in one of the portable lamps or appliances that had been plugged in when the power died. Start plugging them back in one at a time to see what happens. If the fuse blows again immediately after a lamp or other appliance is plugged in, then chances are that that particular lamp (or appliance) has a short in it and is causing the trouble. Or it could be that you have too many appliances plugged into that particular circuit—causing an overload on the fuse or circuit breaker. If the trouble is caused by an overload, the fuse or circuit breaker may not blow immediately—it may take anywhere from one to sixty seconds to blow. The cure for this is obvious—don't plug them all in at the same time or plug some into another circuit.

If all lights in the house or apartment go out at one time, this indicates that one of the main fuses has blown (unless the power supply has been interrupted in your community). This is often a more serious "short" that will require changing the large cartridge fuse and is a problem that is best solved by calling in a professional electrician.

In homes which have circuit breakers instead of fuse boxes, the main "fuse" will also be a circuit breaker—although of much larger capacity than the individual branch circuit breakers. In this case you can safely flick the circuit breaker on again but first try to eliminate the cause of the overload if you can find it—usually by unplugging extra appliances, especially those with large wattage ratings. If this doesn't do the trick, you probably have a short circuit somewhere and should call in an electrician.

CHANGING PLUGS

When a lamp or small portable appliance of any kind fails to work, one of the first things you should suspect is a faulty plug (assuming that you've first checked to make certain the outlet is on if controlled by a wall switch and that a fuse has not blown). First wiggle the plug around in the outlet to see if it is making a good connection. If the lamp flickers or if it comes on only in a certain position then you can usually ensure a permanently good connection by removing the plug from the outlet and then bending the prongs slightly further apart. On plugs that have prongs made of a doubled-over strip of metal, best results will come from inserting a knife blade between the metal leaves as illustrated in figure 72 so as to spread them slightly and thus ensure a tighter fit in the wall outlet.

If the plug's prongs are badly bent, corroded or wobbly; if the plastic or rubber cap is split or a sparking or arcing occurs when you push it in or pull it out of the outlet—then your best bet is to replace the plug entirely. If the plug seems okay, try wiggling the wires around while pushing them in and out where they enter the plug body to see if the insulation is frayed or worn. At the same time you can make certain that the two wires are still solidly connected to the terminals in the plug.

If a new plug is required or if the wires look frayed at the end and seem poorly connected, use a pair of wire-cutting pliers to cut the wire off an inch or two from the plug and attach a new one. Figure 73 illustrates how a conventional plug (the kind with screw terminals near each of the prongs) is installed after first stripping the insulation off each wire with a knife and then feeding the wire through from the back of the plug.

Figure 72: **To ensure a good connection, open spring prongs with a knife as below.**

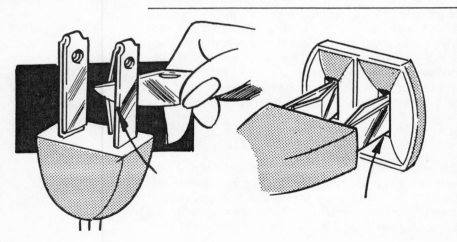

Tie an Underwriter's knot in the two wires as shown in figure 73, then pull the wire back so as to draw the knot down into the recess between the prongs. The purpose of this knot is to take up the strain on the cord when it is yanked—the terminal screws are only designed to make good electrical contact, not to hold the cord in place on the plug. The stranded wires should be twisted tightly and then wrapped around the terminal screws in a clockwise direction so that the wire will be drawn tighter as the screw is tightened. To avoid accidental shorting, make certain that you leave no bare wire ends protruding from under the terminal screws.

Cords on lamps, small radios and other small appliances often are the flat kind that consist of two rubber covered conductors joined together in the middle (often called rip or zip cord). With this type of wire you can use special self-connecting plugs that have no terminal screws and that are much easier to install.

Two of the more popular styles are illustrated in figure 74, but note that each is connected to the wire in approximately the same way: you cut the wire off square without baring the end, then separate the two

Figure 73: **Installing a plug with screw terminals.**

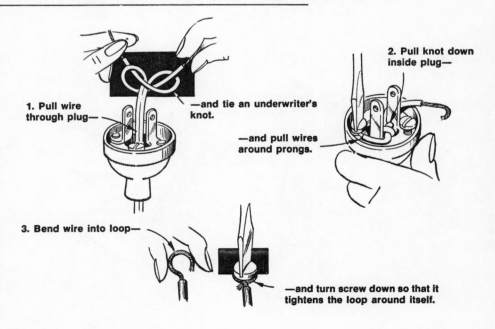

1. Pull wire through plug—

—and tie an underwriter's knot.

—and pull wires around prongs.

2. Pull knot down inside plug—

3. Bend wire into loop—

—and turn screw down so that it tightens the loop around itself.

parts for a distance of about ¼-inch. The wire then fits into the plug which has a set of built-in prongs that penetrate the insulation to make electrical contact when a lever is depressed or when the two parts are forced together. This type of plug is designed for light duty use only with appliances that do not draw a heavy wattage and can only be used with the flat type lamp cord or ripcord.

Figure 74: **Two light-duty self-connecting plugs.**

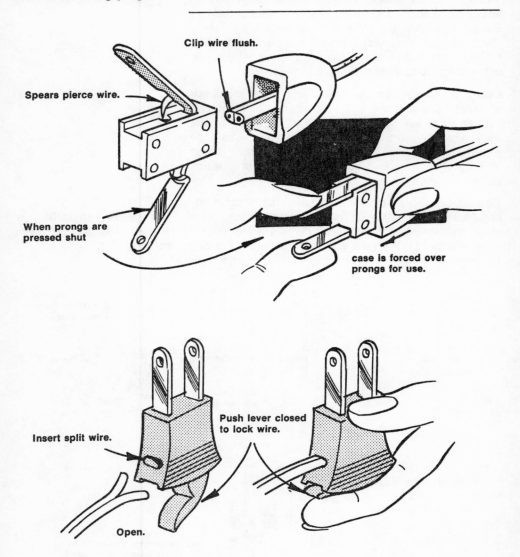

Clip wire flush.

Spears pierce wire.

When prongs are pressed shut

case is forced over prongs for use.

Insert split wire.

Push lever closed to lock wire.

Open.

LAMP CORDS AND SOCKETS

If a floor or table lamp fails to light when you turn the switch on, the most obvious thing to check is the bulb. If this works, make certain that the outlet into which the lamp is plugged is "hot", i.e., that the power is on. If the outlet is controlled by a wall switch, make sure the switch is on; if not check the fuse for that circuit to make certain it is not blown.

If the bulb and the source of power both seem all right, the next thing that should be inspected is the plug on the end of the cord. Try wiggling it around in its outlet in the wall to see if it is loose or if the light blinks, indicating that it is making poor contact (see page 92). Also try wiggling the wires around while the plug is in the wall to see if this causes the light to blink or, even worse, if sparks are visible. Needless to say, if you see sparks pull the plug out immediately. With the plug out of the wall, see if any of the wires have worked loose around the terminal screws or if one of the wires is broken. Also look for insulation that is badly frayed or cracked at any point and inspect the plug itself to see if it is cracked or if any of the metal prongs are loose. If so, remove the plug entirely and replace it with a new one as described on page 93 and 94.

However, if the wire seems old and dried out or if the insulation seems to be worn and cracking, it's a good idea to also replace the entire length of lamp cord at the same time (a new length of lamp cord is advisable if the old cord was too short—it's never a good idea to splice wires together or to use extension cords as a permanent part of the wiring since these introduce one more possible point of failure).

Since lamp cords run in one continuous length from the plug up through the base of the lamp to the lamp socket, the first step is to take apart the lamp socket so that you can disconnect the wires from that end as shown in figure 75. Make certain the plug has been pulled out of the wall to eliminate any danger of shock, then remove the shade and unscrew the bulb. Now if you examine the side of the brass socket near the switch you will see the word "Press" embossed into the metal at one place. Wrap your fingers around the socket, then press hard with your thumb on this point. This will enable you to snap the two parts of the socket apart so that the upper half can be slid off as shown in figure 75. Inside this is a cardboard insulating liner which may come off with it; if not, slide it off separately. This will expose the two terminal screws where the wires are attached.

Pull the socket up out of the lamp base slightly (there's usually enough slack in the wire to permit you to do this) then loosen the terminal screws and disconnect the wires. The bottom half of the socket or cap is screwed onto the threaded end of a little pipe or tube projecting up from the lamp and can be left as is—unless you're going to change the whole socket at the same time.

Figure 75: **Taking apart a lamp socket.**

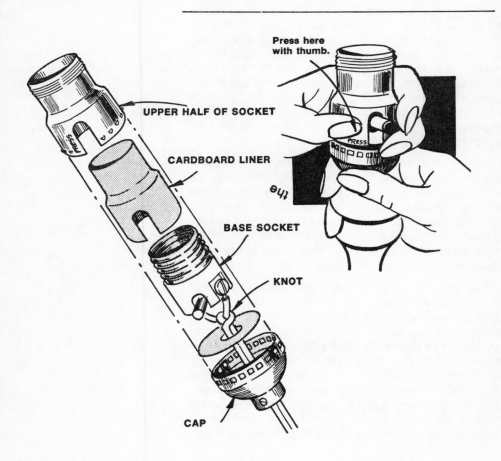

Press here with thumb.

UPPER HALF OF SOCKET

CARDBOARD LINER

BASE SOCKET

KNOT

CAP

You will now be able to pull the old wire out by pulling it from below where it enters through the base of the lamp. Before doing this, tie a heavy piece of string or thin ribbon to the end of the old lamp cord so that as you pull the old wire out you'll pull the string down through the middle of the lamp with it. When the end of the string is pulled out through the base of the lamp you can untie the old wire and tie on the end of the new length of wire so that you can draw it back through the lamp by pulling on the string from the top.

After the new wire comes up through the lamp socket's base, bare the ends by stripping off the insulation with a sharp knife for about ½ inch. Then reconnect these to the two terminals on the socket. Remember to twist the stranded wires tightly before wrapping them around the screw and always wrap them around in a clockwise direction so that the wires will get tighter as you tighten the screws. Now reassemble the socket by slipping the cardboard liner in place, then slide the upper half of the socket down until it snaps into place inside the cap.

REPLACING LAMP SOCKETS AND SWITCHES

Since the switch on most lamps is part of the actual socket, putting in a new switch means replacing the entire socket. Replacement sockets are widely available in all hardware stores and are quite inexpensive, so there's no need to put up with a troublesome lamp switch for long. Remove the old one as described above and replace it with a new one.

In most cases you can leave the base of the socket that's threaded onto the top of the lamp (called the cap) in place since these are made so that most caps on different sockets are interchangeable. If you wish to replace the old cap with a new one, simply unscrew it from the threaded end of the pipe after you have taken the socket apart as illustrated on page 96. On some sockets it may be necessary to loosen a small set screw first (located on the side of the cap) since this set screw "locks" the cap in place to keep it from becoming accidentally unscrewed. To install the new socket you take it apart by unsnapping the top half (see page 96), then install it in reverse order by first pulling the wires through the opening in the bottom of the new cap, then threading it onto the pipe or tube on which the old one fits. Attach the wires to the terminals on the new socket, then reassemble in place on the lamp.

When replacing an old lamp socket you can also select a new one that will give you added conveniences, e.g., you can replace a conventional socket with one that will take three-way bulbs. Or you can buy a lamp socket that has a built-in rotary dimmer switch allowing you to regulate the brightness of the bulb. Either of these come apart and can be installed just like an ordinary lamp socket.

FIXING FLUORESCENT LIGHTS

Fluorescent lamps generally last many times longer than conventional incandescent lamps and use up less electricity for the same amount of illumination, but sooner or later they start to act up—the lamps fail to light all the way across, blink unpredictably, or only work intermittently.

In most cases the trouble is not difficult to correct— providing you are familiar with the simple steps to take in replacing defective components. Figure 76 shows the principal parts of a typical fluorescent lighting fixture and illustrates how they are normally wired together. The ballast is actually a transformer which increases the voltage while the starter is a type of automatic thermal switch that closes momentarily when the current is switched on in order to send current through the filaments at each end of the tube. These filaments then heat mercury vapor inside the tube and this causes the phosphor coating on the inside of the glass to glow—it is this which gives off the light.

After the lamp starts to glow, the starter opens its contacts and shuts off current to the heating part of the filaments but the lamp will continue to glow as long as the current stays on and continues to flow through the ballast. Since very little energy is wasted in heat, fluorescent bulbs give off almost three times as much light per watt of current as an incandescent bulb and they also last a lot longer.

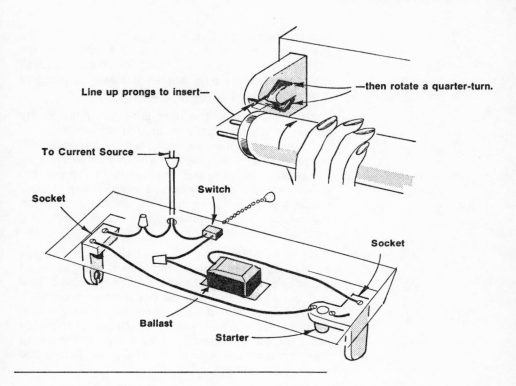

Line up prongs to insert—

—then rotate a quarter-turn.

To Current Source

Socket

Switch

Socket

Ballast

Starter

Much more current is consumed during the initial starting phase (while the starter is preheating the filaments) than while the bulb is on, so that it is cheaper to leave fluorescent lamps burning rather than switching them on and off at frequent intervals. Repeated switching on and off greatly shortens the life of both the lamp and the starter so that more frequent replacement of these parts will be required.

One of the most frequent signs of trouble is blinking or flickering after the lamp is switched on. When this happens—or if one or more tubes fail to light completely—then there are three things that may be wrong: (1) the lamp or tube is not firmly seated in its sockets at each end so that a poor electrical contact is causing the trouble; (2) the starter is defective; or (3) the lamp or tube needs to be replaced with a new one.

To make certain that a poor connection in the socket is not causing the trouble, remove the blinking lamp and then replace it while making certain that the pins are firmly seated at each end (you can do this safely

Figure 76: **A typical fluorescent lighting fixture.**

with the switch on). Line up the pins first, then give the tube a quarter turn to seat it firmly. After it's in, try twisting the tube slightly back and forth to make certain the pins are all the way in and see if this cures the blinking problem.

If this doesn't do it, the next thing to check is the starter which is usually located under one end of the fluorescent tube as indicated in the drawing. Since there's no easy way for you to tell if this gadget is defective, the simplest method is to replace the suspected one with a new one of equal size and capacity. If you don't have a spare on hand, you can borrow one from another fixture which is working satisfactorily.

To remove the starter you'll first have to remove the lamp. Then press the starter inward and give it half a turn in a counterclockwise direction. It should now pull out easily. Put the new one in, then replace the lamp and try again. If the bulb still continues to blink, chances are the bulb itself is wearing out and needs replacing so try inserting a new one of the same size—or test with a bulb from another fixture that is working properly.

A lamp that must be switched on and off several times before it will continue to burn steadily or one whose filaments at the end of the tube continue to glow after the lamp is fully lighted, is usually suffering from a defective starter, so replace it as soon as possible. Also, as tubes start to wear out they gradually blacken near each of the ends. This is normal and does no harm in its early stages—although it cuts down on the amount of light—but it's a good idea to keep new tubes on hand after blackening is first noticed.

Occasionally a fluorescent lamp will not light even though tests indicate that neither the bulb nor the starter is defective. Assuming that the fuse is okay and that the switch which controls the light is not defective, chances are this means that the ballast inside the fixture needs replacing. The only way to check this is to replace it with a new one of equal size and capacity but since this involves internal wiring you may be better off calling an electrician to do the job. If you decide to do it yourself, pull the fuse or shut off the circuit breaker that controls power to that fixture, remove the old ballast and take it with you when you buy a new one that matches. The ballast is usually mounted inside the lighting fixture's box against the back of the plate which holds the lamp sockets and is held in place with two bolts or screws. Before disconnecting the wires that hold the old one in place, mark where each one goes so that you can install the new one and hook it up in exactly the same fashion.

There is one other rarely encountered condition which can cause fluorescent lamps to blink or to glow dimly—excessively low temperatures. This may be a problem when first entering an unheated house or if fluorescent lamps are installed in unheated basements, garages or attics. If temperatures drop much below 60 degrees fluorescent lamps may flicker, blink or burn dimly. Special low temperature bulbs and thermal type starters can help in a condition of this kind but the best solution is to wait till the room warms up.

DOORBELL REPAIRS

When an electric doorbell or chime fails to work properly, nine times out of ten you'll find that the trouble is caused by a faulty pushbutton or a loose or corroded connection at the pushbutton, since this part of the system is subject to the most wear and is the most vulnerable (because it's exposed to the weather). Due to the fact that all home doorbells, buzzers and chimes work on low voltages (10 to 24 volts) you can safely make most repairs without worrying about getting a shock or accidentally blowing a fuse.

When a bell, buzzer, or chime refuses to ring after the button is pushed, remove the pushbutton by unscrewing the mounting screws which hold it in place. Pull the button out from the wall, then check the connections in the back to make certain the two wires are still tightly fastened to the terminal screws on the back and that neither one of the wires is broken. If these seem okay, disconnect the wires entirely, scrape the bare metal clean on each one with a knife blade, then touch the two bared ends together. What you're doing is the same as what the pushbutton is supposed to do when it is pressed—you're closing the circuit. If touching the wires together makes the bell or chime ring, then the trouble is in the button, so replace it with a new one which you can install in place of the old one.

If touching the two wires together at the button did not cause the bell to ring, then the next thing to check is if power (electric current) is being supplied to the bell or chimes. Figure 77a shows a simplified wiring diagram of how the average household doorbell system is connected—either with a single button for the front door or with two buttons, one for the front door and one for a back or side door (see figure 77b). Where there is a two-button system the house will usually be equipped with a combination bell-buzzer (bell for the front door, buzzer for the back door) or with a chime giving two separate tones—one for the front door and one for the back door.

You'll note that the power for each of these systems comes from a transformer that steps the household current (110 volts) down to the necessary low voltage required to operate the bell or chime. In some older

Figure 77a: **A one-door doorbell system.**

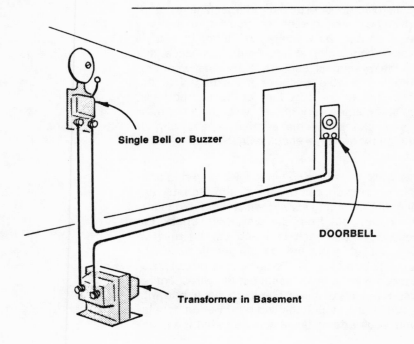

Single Bell or Buzzer

DOORBELL

Transformer in Basement

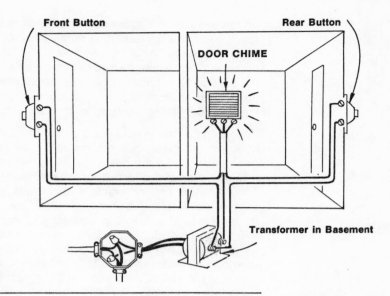

Figure 77b: **A two-door doorbell or chime system.**

houses the bell may still be powered by dry cells or batteries but in modern homes and apartments transformers are almost always used. This transformer is usually mounted somewhere near the main fuse box in the house—it may be screwed directly to the side of the fuse box or it may be mounted on a separate outlet box located on or near the fuse box.

First check to see that the fuse or circuit breaker (which controls the circuit into which the transformer is wired) has not blown. The transformer has two relatively heavy wires coming out of one side which go directly into the outlet box or fuse box and are wired directly into the house current. You should *never* touch these wires (known as the primary wires) since you can get a serious shock from this side of the transformer. The opposite side of the transformer has two terminal buttons or screws to which the wires for the bell system are connected. This is the secondary, low voltage (output) side of the transformer which supplies the 10 or 12 volts needed for the bell.

The transformer is always "on." It is connected to the household system so current always flows through the primary coil. This induces current in the secondary coil so there is always current available on the two terminal screws on the opposite side. You can check this by taking a small piece of wire with each end bared, touching one end to one of the terminal screws while brushing the other end across the second terminal screw on the transformer. Small sparks will indicate that the transformer is still working and delivering current to the system.

If the transformer is delivering current and if a previous test indicates that the trouble was not in the push button, then the next most likely source of the trouble is at the doorbell or chime itself. Take the cover off the bell or chime—sometimes the cover will be held on with a small screw but in most cases it's merely held with spring clips so you can remove it by prying it off. First check to see that the two or three wires are still firmly connected to their terminals and all screws are tight. Then inspect the mechanism of the bell or chime to see if any of the moving parts are obstructed by dirt, dust or accumulated lint that keeps them from moving properly.

In the case of a bell there is a little vibrator mechanism attached to a small ball that acts as a hammer to ring the bell. This should move back and forth freely. If not, see if you can determine what's stopping it. In the case of a chime there are small plastic or metal rods that move up and down or from side to side to strike the chime bars and these too should be free to move easily. If the mechanism seems caked with dust or dirt, you can usually free it up by brushing with a soft artist's brush or by blowing the lint out with the exhaust end of a vacuum cleaner—but do not use oil (see figure 78).

If everything seems okay at this point yet the bell still won't work (in spite of the fact that there seems to be nothing wrong with either the pushbutton or the transformer) then it may be that the bell or chime itself is faulty and needs replacing. The other possibility is that the trouble is being caused by a break in one of the wires somewhere inside the house or in a junction point where the wires meet and are spliced together (usually in the basement almost directly under the bell or chime). Either way, chances are that you'll need an electrician or at least someone quite familiar with electrical repairs to handle the job.

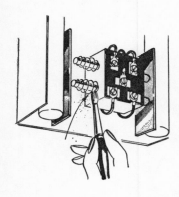

Figure 78: **Clean dust off chimes' push rods with a brush.**

CHAPTER VII

PLUMBING REPAIRS

Clogged sinks, leaky faucets, and other minor plumbing breakdowns always seem to occur late in the evening or at the start of a long weekend when it is virtually impossible to get a plumber (or even the superintendent in an apartment house). Even if you *can* get a professional in, the bill you receive can sometimes convert the smallest plumbing job into a major financial calamity—a 10-cent washer, for example, can cost as much as $15 or $20 by the time you pay for labor and installation by a professional plumber.

Many of these small plumbing jobs are not difficult for you to tackle, providing you are reasonably familiar with the techniques involved. To avoid being caught short when the stores are closed, you will have to make certain that you have spare washers, packing material, pipe sealing compound, and a few other supplies (described later) on hand.

Because emergency repairs may call for quickly shutting off the supply of water to a particular fixture or appliance—or in some cases to the whole house— you should know exactly where the various shut-off valves are located for both hot and cold water supply lines in the home. Every house has one main valve that controls the water supply for the entire building and its location should be familiar to everyone who lives in that house. It is most often located in the basement or utility room right next to the water meter, but if not locate and tag it so that if a break occurs in one of the pipes or if you're in doubt about exactly which supply line is affected when a sudden emergency occurs, you can quickly stop the flow of water and thus ward off a potential flood before much damage has occurred.

In addition to this main valve, every plumbing system should have additional valves located and tagged to permit shutting off the water to individual sinks, tubs or other fixtures. In most modern homes the shut-off valves will be located directly under or behind the sink or fixture, in the basement or even in a closet behind a bathroom or kitchen.

To avoid the confusion that can occur when you're trying to locate the right one in a hurry, the smart thing to do is take time out now while nothing is wrong and find each shut-off valve in the house. Then mark each one with a prominent tag indicating to which fixture (or fixtures) it goes and indicating exactly what line (hot or cold) it controls.

Bear in mind that in addition to water valves there may also be gas valves, steam valves, and hot water heating system valves in various locations—so make sure you tag the right ones. Ideally, every one of these should be tagged so that anyone can find the right one in a hurry when the need arises. It may pay you to call in a plumber and have him identify and mark all the control valves—or call in a knowl-edgeable friend who is familiar with household utility systems.

LEAKING FAUCETS

A faucet that keeps dripping and will not shut off properly can almost always be repaired by simply installing a new washer. As the drawing on page 107 indicates, this washer is located at the end of the valve stem or spindle—the part to which the handle at the top is connected. As you turn the handle the stem threads its way into the faucet body until the washer presses snugly against the valve seat on the inside—thus shutting off the flow of water. If this washer is worn or of improper size and shape, it will not make a tight seal against the valve seat and will permit water to keep dripping out past it. To get at this washer when replacement is needed you'll have to take the faucet apart—a job which should give you no trouble if you take a few minutes to study figure 79 which shows how the various parts fit together.

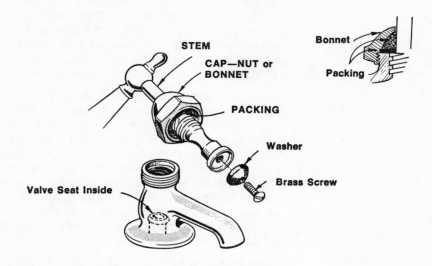

Figure 79: **The parts of a typical faucet.**

Start by first shutting off the water supply to that fixture (if you can't find the right valve, you may have to shut off the main valve for the whole house), then open the faucet until all the water drains out. Next, remove the handle. On some faucets there is a small screw at the top that has to be removed first, after which the handle can be lifted off by tapping upward from the underside. On others the screw that holds the handle in place may be covered by a decorative cap or metal cover which will have to be pried off first with a very small screwdriver or the point of a knife. Some faucets have the handle secured by a small threaded ring or collar (or in some cases a set screw) underneath the handle. Unscrewing this will then permit you to pry or pull the handle off.

After the handle is off, remove the cap-nut or chrome bonnet that fits down on top of the faucet's body and through which the faucet stem projects. This nut or bonnet is threaded onto the faucet body as shown and also serves to hold the packing underneath it (the packing keeps the water from leaking up past or around the stem).

Some kitchen and bathroom faucets have a decorative chrome housing that fits down over the spindle to enclose the packing nut (this serves the same purpose as the cap-nut. On some, the housing and handle are one piece, as illustrated in figure 80. On this type of faucet there will be a nut or bolt which screws down on top of the bonnet or housing to hold it in place. After the housing is removed slide it up over the shaft to expose the packing nut at the bottom.

With either of the styles of faucets just described—the next step is to unscrew the packing nut or cap-nut, then lift and turn out the entire valve stem or spindle. At its bottom end you'll find a small screw holding a rubber or plastic washer in place—usually in a slight recess in the metal. To change the washer, first remove the screw holding it in place, then pry the old washer out carefully. As a rule, you'll find it easier to grip the stem or spindle with a pair of pliers while removing the screws since these screws are sometimes partly corroded or "frozen" in place.

If the screw looks chewed up, replace it at the same time you put in a new washer (brass replacement screws are usually included with the washer assortments that you buy in hardware stores). Replace the washer with a new one of the same size and shape as the old one if you want the faucet to work properly. Some washers are flat while others are tapered and there are several different diameters or sizes in common use. If the washer is so badly chewed up that you can't identify its original shape (flat or conical) then you may have to remove the other faucet on the same sink to find the proper size.

Figure 80: **Taking apart a faucet that has decorative chrome housing instead of a cap-nut.**

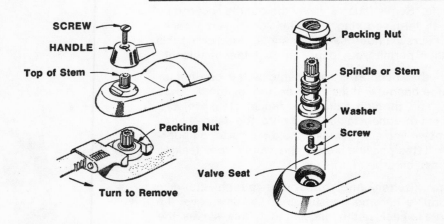

SCREW

HANDLE

Top of Stem

Packing Nut

Turn to Remove

Packing Nut

Spindle or Stem

Washer

Screw

Valve Seat

The faucet is reassembled by screwing the stem or spindle back into the body, then tightening down the packing nut or cap-nut that fits over the top of the spindle. Finish by replacing the decorative chrome housing on those faucets that have one, then install the handle last. If when you originally removed the housing there was putty packed in underneath (often this putty will cover the packing nut so that you have to scrape it away to get at the nut) then it is a good idea to replace it with fresh putty (or glazing compound) before you replace the housing.

If water seems to leak out around the stem of a faucet when it's on (just below the handle) it usually means that either the cap-nut (or packing nut) needs tightening or that the faucet needs new packing under the cap-nut. The first thing to do is to try tightening the cap-nut or packing nut slightly with a large flat-jaw wrench, such as a monkey wrench. If tightening this doesn't do the trick—or if you have to tighten it so much that the handle becomes too hard to turn easily—then the faucet needs new packing.

As described on page 107, the packing is under the cap-nut or bonnet on most older style faucets. However, on many modern faucets with decorative chrome housings around the spindie the packing will be under the packing nut (see figure 80).

In either case, to replace this packing shut off the water supply to the fixture, then take the faucet apart the same as you would for replacing the washer. Use the blade of a small screwdriver to dig out all of the old packing and replace it with new material. This packing comes in a string-like form which you wrap around the stem and then force back into the cavity under the cap-nut or packing nut. Put enough in to completely fill the cavity under the packing nut or cap nut, but not so much as to interfere with threading it back into place.

If a faucet continues to drip after a new washer has been inserted, or if washers seem to wear out exceptionally fast, chances are the valve seat on the inside (see figure 80) (the piece against which the washer presses) is damaged. Most hardware stores sell inexpensive valve seat grinders or seat-dressing tools which you can use to smooth off a roughened valve seat. These have a stem or handle which you screw into the faucet in place of the original valve stem so that the grinding end of the tool bears down against the valve seat. A matching bonnet nut on this tool holds the shaft in place in the faucet body while you give it two or three turns to remove nicks or scratches on the valve's seat. After this grinding or dressing action unscrew the tool, blow or wipe out any particles left on the inside, then replace the original valve stem and washer assembly.

SINGLE-CONTROL VALVE FAUCETS

Modern single-handle (also called single-control) faucets have only one handle that regulates the proportion of hot and cold water as well as the volume. They have no washers or washer seats that can wear down—hence there is much less of a problem with drips or leaks developing and much less over-all maintenance required.

However, single-handle faucets have some moving parts that eventually wear out and permit leaks to develop (although this may take years in normal home use) so repairs will be required sooner or later. In the earliest models this was quite often a complicated job since there were many different types of construction in use, most requiring almost complete disassembly in order to make the needed repairs. But nowadays there are only a comparatively few styles in wide-spread use and the four or five large manufacturers in this field have designed their units so that the heart of each valve mechanism is an easily replaceable cartridge or ball unit that can be purchased from plumbing supply dealers when one of these faucets develops a leak.

Basically, washerless single-handle faucets differ from standard faucets (with washers) in that the flow of water is not controlled by a rubber washer pressing against a metal surface (the valve seat). Instead there is an eccentric-type valve—or it may be a sliding or tipping valve—which is designed so that as it is moved it slides past (or tips against) an opening on the inside to open or close it (all or part-way). In one direction this valve permits more hot water to enter, in the other more cold water—when furthest to one side there is only hot water; to the other, only cold water.

At the same time the unit is arranged so that the valve or mixing mechanism can move in another direction—in and out or back and forth—without disturbing the relative amount of hot and cold water that is allowed to enter, and it is this second movement that controls the total volume of water that comes out through the spout. Most are designed so that after the temperature has been adjusted, the faucet can be shut off or the volume regulated without affecting the temperature setting.

When a washer or packing is needed for a conventional faucet, you can usually find the needed parts at your local hardware store—not so with single-control faucets. Because of the variety of brands on the market (each requiring its own parts) and because few do-it-yourselfers have had occasion to repair their own single-handle faucets, parts for these units are seldom stocked by local hardware stores—unless they happen to specialize in plumbing supplies. The parts will have to be purchased from a specialized plumbing supply house—usually the type that caters primarily to the professional plumber. It must be kept in mind that these houses do not necessarily carry all brands—if the dealer sells only Brand A single-control faucets, he will only carry Brand A's repair parts, so you may have to shop more than one supply house to find the replacement unit you need.

Replacement cartridges or balls almost always come with an instruction sheet and an "exploded" view of the faucet showing how the various parts fit together and explaining how the faucet must be taken apart to remove the worn parts and install the new ones. When any of these start to drip or do not control the flow of water properly, it is the cartridge or ball assembly that must be replaced. The first step is to shut off both the hot and cold water supplies (if there are no valves for this under the sink then there should be some in the basement—otherwise the main valves will have to be closed).

The next step is to remove the handle, usually held in place by a small screw (on some models this screw will be covered by a decorative escutcheon plate or cap). Parts should then be carefully removed in the order shown on the instruction sheet and laid out neatly, preferably in the same order, so that they can be replaced without mixing them up. Some repair kits will include O-rings that should be put in at the same time, although not all models have these. On kitchen faucets it will usually be necessary to remove the spout, which simple lifts off—while on bathroom lavatories, this will seldom be required.

Although all this may sound a bit complicated to the uninitiated, the job is relatively simple if you are even moderately familiar with plumbing repairs—providing you have the instruction sheet or parts diagram to follow and providing the right parts are purchased. If you don't have the one that originally came with the unit, write to the manufacturer or check the phone book to find the nearest distributor (a trademark or company symbol is usually engraved on the faucet).

Kitchen faucets equipped with a swivel spout will sometimes develop leaks around the base of the swiveling section but in many cases this is due to worn O-rings on the inside. They are easily replaced by removing the handle and then lifting off the spout but it is important that the new ones be exactly the same size as the old ones.

Another problem that sometimes occurs is loss of volume or flow: if this happens or if the spray attachment fails to work properly (on kitchen faucets equipped with a dishwasher spray), then check the aerator, i.e., the little screen that screws onto the end of the spout. If it becomes partially clogged with sediment it will cut down the pressure and interfere with the diverter valve that directs water to the spray. To clean it, flush under a strong stream of water while holding it upside down and scrub with a small, stiff brush (an old toothbrush works well).

CLOGGED SINK DRAINS

Although sinks sometimes become clogged because a foreign object is accidentally dropped down the drain, the trouble is usually caused by ignoring the fact that the sink was actually draining sluggishly for days—or even weeks—before it stopped up completely.

In kitchen sinks the majority of stoppages are caused by accumulations of grease which cake up in the trap (the U-shaped piece of pipe in the drain directly below the sink). As grease accumulates and hardens, it traps small patricles of food and other solid waste such as coffee grounds, vegetable peelings and the like—until finally a sizable obstruction builds up. You can obviously avoid most stoppages of this kind by not letting materials go down the drain that could cause trouble.

For example, instead of pouring waste grease or fat into the sink, pour it into a can or other container, allow to cool, then dispose of it along with your other garbage. In addition, coffee grounds, food crumbs, peelings and other solid matter should be kept out of the drain whenever possible and the sink strainer should never be removed while the sink is in use. Anything that won't fit through the small holes in the strainer does not belong in the drain pipe.

In bathroom sinks and tubs the most common culprit is hair, combined in many cases with a build-up of soap curds. Most modern bathroom sinks have built-in metal stoppers that can be opened or closed by raising or lowering (depending on the design) a knob or handle behind the spout. The actual stopper is a metal cap that raises up into the sink when the drain is open, then closes down for a snug fit against the metal-rimmed drain opening when closed.

As can be seen in figures 81, 82, and 83, the stopper is connected by a linkage that moves it up or down when the handle at the top is moved and the end of this linkage projects into the drain pipe opening to actuate the stopper. It is in this area that hair is often trapped until it builds up to the point where it obstructs (or partially obstructs) drainage. The matted hair also serves to catch soap that sometimes cakes up and further adds to the obstruction.

On most sinks the stopper can be removed by simply raising it as far as it will go, then twisting it about one-half a turn after which it should lift out. If this doesn't work, you may have to unfasten the stopper by working from below. Unscrew the packing nut or

Figure 81: **Metal-stopper linkage in bathroom sink.**

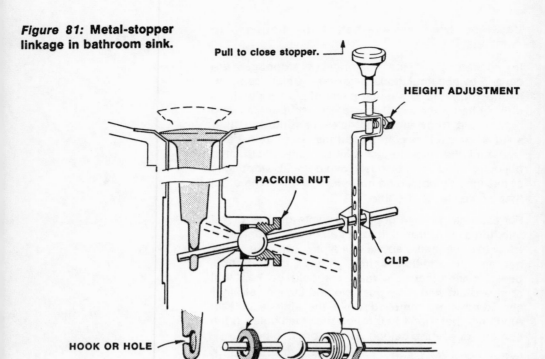

Pull to close stopper.

HEIGHT ADJUSTMENT

PACKING NUT

CLIP

HOOK OR HOLE

Figure 82: **Another metal-stopper linkage.**

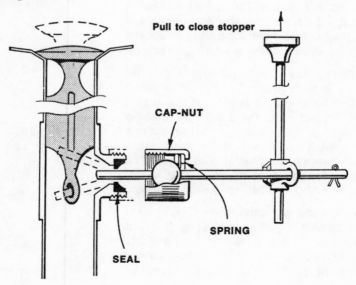

Pull to close stopper

CAP-NUT

SPRING

SEAL

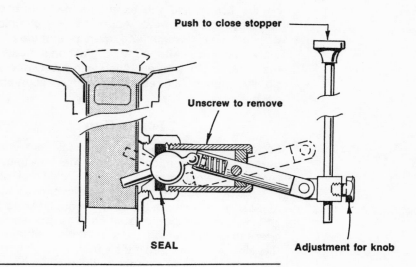

Push to close stopper

Unscrew to remove

SEAL

Adjustment for knob

Figure 83: **Yet another metal-stopper linkage.**

cap-nut through which the connecting arm fits (see drawings) as it enters the drain pipe, then pull out the rod with the nut that holds it in place. This enables you to lift the stopper out from the top so that you can clean off hair and lint that may have accumulated around it. Stoppers in bathtubs can be lifted out in the same way—that is, by grasping them and turning slightly to free them from the linkage.

Chemical Cleaners

If a sink drain acts sluggish even though there is no hair trapped around the metal stopper—or no grease or other foreign matter trapped around the sink strainer—you should try a chemical drain cleaner, following the manufacturer's directions. (It's also a good idea to use drain cleaner as a preventive measure every two or three months).

Remember that these drain cleaners are usually quite caustic, so wear rubber gloves and be careful about spilling them anywhere except inside the drain. They should not be used when the sink is full of water nor should they be used in hot water. If the fixture is already quite full, then dip most of the water out first so that you can pour the compound directly into the drain opening without allowing it to come in contact with the porcelain finish. Depending on the brand and the extent of the stoppage, you may have to wait several hours for the chemical to work its way through and even repeat the process more than once. After a gurgling action indicates that the drain is fully open, flush with plenty of water to rid the pipe of all remaining caustic solution.

Force Cup

For complete stoppages or for those that can't be cured with a chemical cleaner, the tool to use is a rubber force cup or plunger (often called a plumber's helper). Before starting, make certain there is at least some water in the sink—enough to completely cover the rubber cup when it is pressed down over the drain opening. If it's a kitchen sink remove the sink strainer first; if it's a bathroom sink remove the metal or rubber stopper by lifting it out completely. Place the rubber cup firmly over the drain opening while holding a damp cloth pressed tightly against the overflow opening near the top rim of the sink (in bathroom basins), then press down firmly with a hard push to create pressure in the line and immediately jerk the handle back upward to create a suction action right after the compression stroke (see figure 84).

Repeat this up-and-down motion five or six times, then yank the cup up from the opening to see if the water starts to drain away. Remember that in most cases the suction (up) stroke of the force cup is actually more effective in breaking up the clog than the compression (down) stroke; so place extra emphasis on yanking the handle up each time after making certain that the rim of the cup is in firm contact with the sink bottom before you start. Plugging the overflow opening in a bathtub or kitchen sink with a damp rag is essential—otherwise the energy expanded by the force cup will be wasted in forcing water and air out through this opening rather than down through the drain pipe.

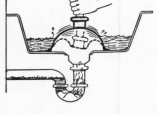

Figure 84: **The upward pull of the force cup is often best for removing stoppage.**

Using a Plumber's Snake

If none of these methods work, the trouble may be due to the fact that the trap or drain pipe underneath or behind the fixture is clogged with something solid that will have to be physically removed by using a plumber's snake or drain auger. This is a long piece of flexible spring steel or tightly coiled wire that you can push down through the pipe to break up or remove obstructions. It will have a coiled spring-wire tip that is sharp enough to work its way through clogs or hook into foreign objects so that you can pull them through the drain pipe opening.

Figures 85 and 86 show the two most common types of sink traps (these are directly below the sink and connected to the lower end of the sink's drain pipe). Both are U-shaped so that they hold liquid at the bottom and thus keep noxious odors from filtering up through the sink drain. Some have a clean-out plug at the bottom and some do not. The ones that don't are easily removable by loosening the two retaining nuts which hold them in place as shown. The other type of trap must be removed by unscrewing it from the pipe that projects out from the wall but the clean-out plug at the bottom usually eliminates the need for this.

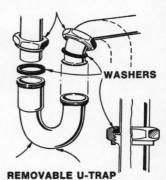

RETAINING NUTS

WASHERS

REMOVABLE U-TRAP

Figure 85: **Most common type of sink trap. Some have clean out plugs in trap, some do not.**

Figure 86: **Older type sink trap screws onto waste pipe in wall.**

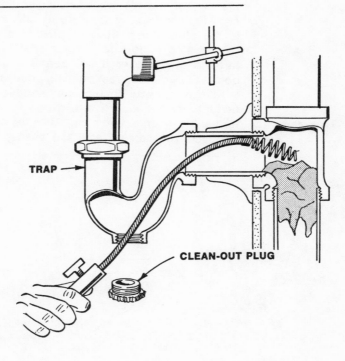

TRAP →

CLEAN-OUT PLUG

Place a pail or a large pan under the trap, then use a wrench to remove the clean-out plug (if there is one). If there is no clean-out plug, remove the entire U-shaped piece as shown by loosening the two large retaining nuts which hold it in place at each end. Slide the nuts back up out of the way but be sure you don't lose the rubber washers or gaskets that fit inside them. Allow all water trapped in the drain to flow out into the pail or pan that you have placed underneath, then probe the inside of the trap and up through the drain opening with the end of your snake to see if there are any obstructions.

If both the sink drain and the trap are clear, then the obstruction is obviously in the pipe leading into the wall or floor, so start probing with your snake (see figure 87). Keep pushing it into the wall a few inches at a time, occasionally pulling it back slightly while turning or twisting the handle end. The steel snake is flexible enough to go around bends and sharp turns, although you may have to exert a little extra pressure when you come to a joint.

When you feel an obstruction, maintain pressure on the end of the tool while twisting so as to cause the hook or coiled spring at the tip to bite into the clog in the pipe. Either this will push it out of the way by breaking it up into small pieces that will flush through the pipe or it will permit you to draw the object through the drain opening under the sink. As a rule, when you do feel an obstruction it is always better to try and pull it out, rather than pushing it *Figure 87: Two ways to* further down into the pipe. After the obstruction is *use a snake.* removed, you can reinstall the U-shaped trap and

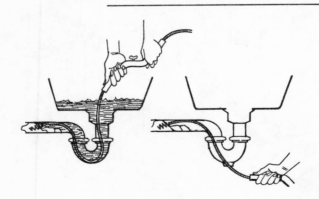

clean-out plug, but be sure you thread the retaining nuts and the plug on carefully since these have fine brass threads that are easily damaged by forcing if the pieces are not precisely in line.

CLOGGED TOILETS

Toilet bowls do not have separate traps underneath them the way sinks and other fixtures do—the trap is built in as part of the fixture (see figure 88). When water and other material is flushed out of the bowl it has to run up and over a protruding lip which serves to always keep a certain amount of water trapped in the bottom of the bowl.

Because toilet bowls have very large drain openings which normally do not obstruct easily (it takes a sizable mass to block these drains), chemical cleaners are seldom effective on clogged toilets. A rubber force cup or plunger can often be used but on some models the opening is too large or not shaped properly to permit you to cover the opening with the bottom end of the cup. However, if the shape or design of your toilet bowl permits you to apply suitable pressure with a force cup, this is almost always the easiest method to try first—following the same technique as you would on a sink drain.

For more serious toilet stoppages, a plumber's snake or drain auger is the tool you will need. Because of the built-in trap on a toilet bowl, using a snake or auger is a bit more difficult since it takes considerable pressure to force the snake into and through the trap area. Twisting steadily on the handle end while maintaining pressure on the other end will usually do the trick (see figure 88). But if you have trouble forcing the end of the snake or auger past the trap, slip a plastic garbage bag over your hand and your arm, then push your hand under the water and guide the tip of the snake past the inside rim of the trap. The extra pressure you can apply on the tip in this way should be enough to push the snake through. Keep feeding and twisting the snake downward until you feel the clog, then twist and pull repeatedly until you either pull the obstruction out or break it up enough to permit the water to flow out past it.

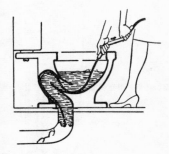

Figure 88: **Clearing a toilet bowl of stoppage with a snake.**

In very extreme cases when none of these methods work, the only way to clean out the line is to remove the toilet bowl entirely so you can get at the drain pipe underneath. Unfortunately this job usually calls for the services of a professional plumber.

TOILET TANK REPAIRS

Nine times out of ten when the flush tank on your toilet keeps on running or fails to flush properly the repairs required are surprisingly simple to make and may involve only the purchase of an inexpensive part. These repairs are simple if you are reasonably familiar with how a toilet tank works so that you can follow an intelligent plan in locating the source of the trouble—to the uninitiated the inside of a flush toilet tank may look like a Rube Goldberg contraption that only a master engineer would dare monkey with.

Figure 89: **Working mechanism of a flush-type toilet tank.**

Figure 89 illustrates the working mechanism of a typical flush-type toilet tank (the kind you probably have in your home or apartment) viewed from the front as though the front side of the tank has been cut

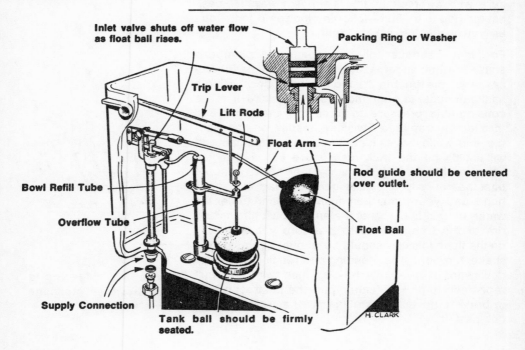

Inlet valve shuts off water flow as float ball rises.

Packing Ring or Washer

Trip Lever

Lift Rods

Float Arm

Rod guide should be centered over outlet.

Bowl Refill Tube

Overflow Tube

Float Ball

Supply Connection

Tank ball should be firmly seated.

H. CLARK

away to give you a look at the inside. If you start
with the assumption that the tank is now full of water
("full" means that the water level is just below the
top of the overflow tube), below is a brief explanation
of how the various parts function.

When you press down on the handle on the outside,
the trip lever on the inside raises—pulling the lift
rods upward. This raises the rubber tank ball off its
seat at the bottom and permits the water in the tank
to rush rapidly out through the opening and into the
bowl to flush it.

As the water level inside the flush tank starts dropping rapidly, the large metal or plastic float ball at
the top drops with it. This ball is connected by a
float arm to the inlet valve assembly (called a ballcock). As the arm drops it automatically opens the
inlet valve at the top of the ballcock and water comes
rushing in to refill the tank. (To minimize splashing,
this water actually comes out through the tube at
the side which points down toward the bottom of
the tank.) Since the rubber tank ball at the bottom
is hollow and has air trapped underneath, it tends
to float rapidly upward as soon as it is raised off
its seat by the lift rod, even though you let go of
the handle on the outside. As the water level drops,
this ball falls back down until it once again sits firmly
against the valve seat at the bottom—once more
sealing the opening that leads out to the toilet bowl.

When the water rushing through the inlet valve starts
to accumulate, it presses the tank ball down to form
a tight seal which keeps the water from running back
into the toilet bowl. As the water level inside the tank
rises, the float ball and its arm also rise with it until
a predetermined level is reached. As it rises the float
arm actuates a mechanism inside the inlet valve
(ballcock) that shuts off the water when the tank is
full and ready for the next flushing action (see figure
90).

While the tank is refilling, part of the water coming
through the inlet valve is diverted through the flexible
bowl refill tube so that it flows down through the
overflow tube into the toilet bowl. This refills the trap
in the bottom of the bowl and restores the water
level inside the toilet.

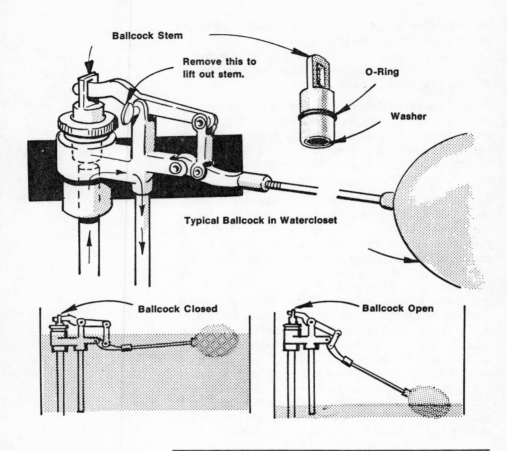

Ballcock Stem

Remove this to lift out stem.

O-Ring

Washer

Typical Ballcock in Watercloset

Ballcock Closed

Ballcock Open

Figure 90: **Ballcock action.**

Water Keeps Running

Probably the most common toilet problem is when water continues running from the tank into the bowl after flushing is complete. When this happens, the first thing to do is take the tank cover off and look inside to see if the tank is full or empty.

If the tank is almost empty and water keeps running in without the tank ever refilling properly, then chances are that the tank ball at the bottom is not seating properly against its valve seat so that water keeps leaking continuously past it into the toilet bowl. There are two things that can cause this: the rubber ball is worn, especially along the bottom, and can no longer form a firm seal against the seat; or it does not seat properly because the guide rod which lifts it is not properly centered over the valve seat opening (so that when the ball falls back down it doesn't fall over the center of the valve seat).

If the ball is worn—or even if you're in doubt about it—replace it with a new one (they're cheap). This rubber ball is simply screwed onto the bottom of the lift rod, thus to replace it unthread the old one and screw the new one back in its place. Although you can do this while the tank has water in it, you'll probably find it easier to shut off the water supply to the tank. In most homes there is a shut-off valve located directly under the tank, otherwise you may have to turn off the appropriate valve in the basement. After shutting off the valve, flush the tank once to empty it so you can then work on the inside while the tank is dry.

If the original rubber tank ball seems in good condition—or if you've recently replaced it with a new one and it still does not seat properly, then you'll probably have to move the rod guide slightly to one side or the other in order to center the ball over its seat. Most of these guides have a set screw which clamps them in place around the outside of the overflow tube as indicated in the drawing, so by loosening this screw slightly you can swing the guide arm left or right until the ball falls directly over the center of the valve seat when allowed to drop.

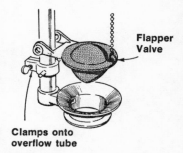

Flapper Valve

Clamps onto overflow tube

One permanent way to eliminate the problem of having to worry about alignment of the tank ball with its seat is to replace the tank ball with one of the new flapper valves similar to the one illustrated in figure 91. This needs no guide rods or guide arm—you remove these old parts entirely. To raise the hinged rubber flapper (which clamps around the overflow tube) you attach the length of chain supplied directly to the trip lever arm as shown.

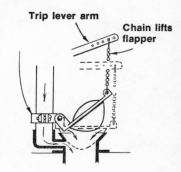

Trip lever arm

Chain lifts flapper

If after lifting the cover from a tank that keeps running continuously you find that the tank is full and the water keeps running out through the top of the overflow tube, this means that the inlet valve is not shutting off as it should after the water reaches its proper level inside the tank. As a result, it keeps overflowing into the toilet bowl through the overflow tube—either in a steady stream or in the form of a persistent trickle. When this happens, there are

Figure 91: **The flapper valve.**

two things to check: the float ball and arm, or the ballcock (this is the part that contains the inlet valve which controls the flow of water into the tank).

To find out which one is causing the trouble, try lifting up the float ball by raising it as high as it will go. If this stops the flow of water into the tank, unscrew the float ball from the end of its arm and shake it to see if there is water on the inside. If so, the ball has developed a leak and does not float up as high as it should, so you'll have to replace it.

If the ball is not leaking (it has no water on the inside) then the trouble may be caused by improper adjustment of the float arm. In other words, the arm does not allow the ball to rise high enough to shut the water off before it reaches the level of the overflow pipe opening. The simplest way to make this adjustment is to bend the float arm slightly downward near the middle (this float arm is made of soft metal so that you can bend it with your hands). Bending it downward will make it shut off sooner—lowering the level at which the water in the tank is maintained. Experiment with this adjustment until the float shuts off the water when its level rises almost—but not quite—to the top of the overflow pipe. Many tanks have a line drawn against the back on the inside to show the proper water level when full.

If lifting up on the float ball and arm does not shut off the flow of water from the inlet valve into the tank, then the trouble is in the ballcock mechanism itself. This unit has a washer on the inside as well as one or more packing rings or O rings that eventually wear and need replacing (see drawing on page 122). Most ballcocks can be disassembled and repaired but even professional plumbers agree that when trouble develops in one they are usually so old and worn that it's simpler and quicker to replace the entire ballcock with a new one that will also be quieter and more efficient in operation than your old one was.

Since this is a job that involves disconnecting the water supply at the bottom of the tank, you may prefer to call in a plumber—although it's not a very difficult task which you could safely handle yourself. The job should take less than an hour and the only tools you'll need are a few wrenches and a pair of pliers. Most new ballcock assemblies come complete with all necessary fittings and installation instructions.

However, if you decide to tackle the job yourself it's a good idea to do it on a day when the hardware stores are open so that if you find you need an additional part you can run down and get it without having to leave your toilet tank completely disassembled—and be without toilet facilities—until the following day or for an entire weekend.

NOISY PLUMBING

Hammering, banging, chattering or squealing noises in your household plumbing system can be caused by many different things which should be corrected as soon as possible—not only to eliminate frayed nerves but to prevent the possibility of a serious breakdown in the future. The hammering and banging causes vibration in the pipes that could eventually result in loose joints or ruptured fittings, especially if the trouble is caused by loose or missing mounting straps or clamps.

One of the most common noises is a whistling or squealing sound that you hear every time you turn on a faucet. This may be accompanied by a chattering noise that gradually disappears as the faucet is fully opened. If it only happens in one faucet and only when it's being turned on, then chances are that the trouble is caused by wear inside the faucet itself. In many cases a new washer on the inside is all that's required (see page 108).

If the washer is not the cause of the trouble—if the old one is still in good shape or if putting in a new one doesn't stop the noise—then it's likely that the threads on the faucet spindle are badly worn or otherwise damaged so that there is an excess amount of play inside the faucet. One test that indicates this is the problem is to open the faucet halfway and try to wiggle the handle around. If there is more play in this handle than there is in other faucets in the house, the spindle thread is probably worn and causing the trouble. If so, remove the spindle and stem entirely (see page 108), then take this down to your local plumbing supply dealer to see if you can buy a replacement. Otherwise an entirely new facuet will have to be purchased and installed—usually a job for an experienced plumber.

Sometimes you'll hear a chattering or banging noise in your plumbing because several of the mounting straps or supports that hold the pipes in place have worked loose. This is something you may or may not be able to fix—depending on where the trouble is. First try inspecting all of the exposed lengths of pipe in the house—especially in the basement, crawl spaces or other unfinished areas where the pipes are easily seen. Look for any place where a pipe strap seems to have pulled loose or where there is a lot of sagging and vibration that you can feel when the water is running.

As a rule, water pipes should be supported at 6 to 8 foot intervals, as well as near all elbows and other fittings. You can install additional mounting straps yourself by simply nailing or screwing them in place against studs or beams across which the pipe passes (see figure 92). If the trouble is inside a wall then the problem is complicated by the fact that someone will have to rip the wall open in order to get at the loose pipe—definitely a job for a professional.

If the hammering or banging noise only occurs when a faucet is turned off, then chances are that the problem is caused by a condition known as "water hammer." To cure this there are special anti-hammer devices which plumbers can install to absorb the shock each time a faucet is suddenly shut off (particularly a problem with washing machine faucets where the water is turned on and off repeatedly by electric valves inside the machine). Since water cannot be compressed, its momentum causes it to slam forward and bang against the pipe walls when the flow is suddenly stopped. Anti-hammer devices have an air chamber that acts as a pneumatic shock absorber. They provide a "cushion" of air that will soak up the extra energy created by the rushing water and thus eliminate the hammering effect that would otherwise occur.

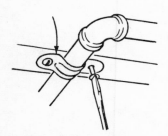

Figure 92: **Strap pipe to ceiling joist at six-foot intervals.**

SHOWER HEADS

Accumulations of sediment or corrosion in water lines will sometimes clog shower heads and create a poorly dispersed spray. Sometimes merely opening and closing the adjustment (assuming you have an adjustable spray head) will do the trick. Otherwise, remove the shower head entirely by unscrewing it from the pipe which projects from the wall. When doing this, be sure you hold the pipe with a small pipe wrench or pair of pliers while you twist the shower head off with another pair of pliers—otherwise you may loosen the pipe inside the wall. When you have the shower head off you might try cleaning the openings with a toothpick or fine piece of stiff wire. If this doesn't work then your best bet is to buy a new one—it is installed by merely twisting it back on in place of the old one. Be sure to tighten it firmly as you again hold the pipe with a separate wrench or pair of pliers to keep it from twisting.

CHAPTER VIII

FLOORS AND STAIRS

Floors or steps that squeak and creak every time someone walks on them, or loose boards that cause people to trip up or down a flight of stairs are great for laughs and/or atmosphere in a television show or movie but they can be quite unfunny in your own home or apartment. Yet it is only in a comparatively few instances that major carpentry, beyond the scope of the average home handywoman, will be required. Here are problems that you're most likely to encounter with your wood floors and stairs, as well as with other popular types of floors and floor coverings . . . and the solutions for each.

SQUEAKY FLOORS

A wood floor that squeaks or makes creaking noises everytime someone walks across a certain section is almost always due to one or more loose boards that move up and down when stepped upon. The boards may have loosened because the floor beams underneath have warped, because floor boards have buckled, because some of the nails have worked loose or because the flooring was not properly nailed and installed in the first place.

Practically all of the flooring in current use consists of tongue-and-groove boards which are nailed down along one edge (the tongue edge). When someone steps on one of these boards that has worked loose or buckled upwards, its edge rubs against the edge of the board next to it (or it may rub against the sub-flooring underneath), and this causes the squeaking or creaking noises that you hear.

To stop this kind of noise and silence the boards there are two things that one can do: (1) You can lubricate the joint between the boards so that they slide against each other without making the rubbing noise that causes the creaking; or (2) you can tighten or fasten the loose boards down so they will no longer be able to move whenever someone steps on them.

The first method will get rid of the noise without actually correcting the basic cause and it will work in most cases—but this cure is only a temporary one since the lubricant will eventually wear off and the squeaking will start again. The second method will eliminate the problem entirely and thus cure it permanently—providing the job is done properly.

If you want to try the first method—lubrication—there are several kinds of lubricant you can use: dry powdered graphite (the same kind is used for lubricating locks), non-staining white powdered lubricant which some hardware stores stock for use on sliding doors and windows—or even ordinary talcum powder. Once you've located the offending board or boards, you squirt or blow the powder down between the edges of the boards while someone steps on and off them to help the material work its way into the joint. After one or two tries the squeaking should stop.

This is merely a temporary cure—to permanently eliminate the problem the loose boards should be tightened by use of nails or screws in order to keep them from moving every time someone steps on them. The trick here is to drive your nails or screws in the right place—and in order to do this you have to have some idea of how a typical wood floor is constructed. Figure 93 shows a cross section of a typical floor. There are large beams, called joists, which support the flooring. On top of this are (usually) two layers of boards—the subflooring which runs across the joists (either at right angles to the joists or at a 45-degree angle) and the finished flooring which is nailed down on top of this.

Squeaks can be caused by loose boards in either the subflooring or the finished flooring but in either case the procedure is the same: first locate the area where the boards are loose, then nail or screw the boards down so that they cannot move. Have someone walk around on the floor while you watch and listen to try and determine exactly where the trouble

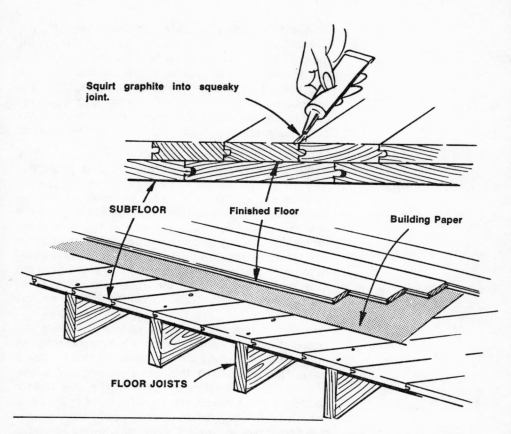

Squirt graphite into squeaky joint.

SUBFLOOR   Finished Floor   Building Paper

FLOOR JOISTS

spot is. Then, while your "assistant" stands on top of the loose boards (to hold them down) you drive two 3-inch finishing nails in at an angle to each other so that they almost form a "V" as shown in figure 94. Crossing them in this way will make them grip better with less likelihood of their pulling out.

Figure 93: **A typical floor.**

Figure 94: **One way to secure loose floor boards.**

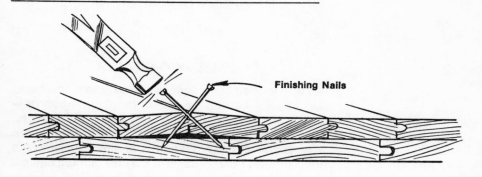

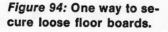

Finishing Nails

To avoid damaging the floor with your hammer, it's a good idea to drive the nails most of the way in, then finish by using a nailset to drive the heads below the surface. If your floors are oak the hardness of the wood may make it difficult to drive the nails without bending them, so drill a small pilot hole first (slightly smaller than the diameter of the nail) to simplify hammering and to minimize the likelihood of splitting the wood.

If the loose boards are in the finished floor, this method should anchor the boards down to the subflooring so that they will no longer move. If it is the subflooring that is loose, this method will only work if you can drive your nails into one of the floor joists rather than merely through the flooring. If the floor is unfinished from below (such as in an unfinished basement) then you can locate the joists by measuring out from one of the walls on the underside of the floor, then duplicating this measurement on top of the floor.

However, if the ceiling below is finished, then the simplest way to locate the joists is to tap across the surface of the flooring with a block of wood and a hammer. Keep doing this while moving the block around and you'll notice that there is a dull hollow sound in most places when you're tapping between the joists. However, when you're directly over a joist the sound will be much more solid—this is where you want to drive your nails. Bear in mind that floor joists are usually spaced at 16-inch intervals and that the finished flooring will often run parallel to these joists since the subflooring usually runs across them. Any holes left when the nail heads are countersunk can be filled afterward by using a colored wood plastic that matches the finish of your floor.

SQUEAKY STAIRS

As with a wood floor, squeaks in wooden staircases are usually caused by one or more loose boards— in this case a loose tread (the part you step on). The tread may be loose along the front edge where it rests on top of its riser (this is the vertical piece that supports the tread) or it may be rubbing against the stringer at the sides (the stringer is the piece that runs along each side of the stairway supporting both the treads and risers).

Here again there are two ways to get rid of the noise: by lubricating with powdered graphite, talcum powder or similar lubricant, or by fastening down the loose piece so it can no longer move and thus rub against other members. If you decide to try a lubricant, squirt or blow it into the joints between the tread and the riser and between the tread and the stringer along the side. Step up and down on the tread a few times, then repeat the process once or twice until the noise ceases.

To tighten the loose tread and thus get rid of the problem permanently, the easiest method is to drive a few nails in from the top as indicated in figure 95. These should be driven in at an angle with alternate nails sloping in opposite directions when viewed from the front. You'll notice that every tread overhangs the riser slightly at the front, so be sure you locate the nails far enough back so that they go into the top edge of the riser, yet not so far back that they miss it completely. The easiest way to do this is to measure under the nose of the tread to see how far it protrudes from the face of the riser; then before driving your nails, space them about ⅜ inch further from the front so they will be approximately in center of the vertical riser. Have someone stand on top of the tread to hold it down while you're hammering.

For an even stronger repair use long #8 screws instead of nails, drilling pilot holes first—selecting a drill bit that is about the same diameter as the body of the screw (without the threads). The pilot hole should go through the tread and down into the edge of the riser. Rub the tip of the screw on a cake of soap or paraffin to help lubricate the threads before you drive the screw into the hole and countersink the screw heads slightly (set them below the surface) so that you can cover them up afterward with colored wood plastic or putty.

On stairs going down to the basement or on other stairways where the underside is open and exposed, you can make repairs by working from below. On many stairs of this kind you'll note that there are wedges along the sides where the treads fit into notches in the stringers, and these may have worked

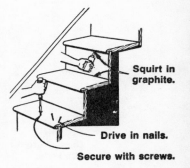

Squirt in graphite.

Drive in nails.

Secure with screws.

Figure 95: **Three ways to silence squeaking stairs.**

loose. If so, pry them out, coat them with glue, then hammer them back in until they are snug. While examining the underside of an exposed staircase you may also find that the bottom edge of the riser has become separated from the tread below it because of constant kicking as people walk up the stairs. To correct this, hammer the riser against the tread, then drive a few nails or screws through the riser and into the edge of the tread to hold it in place.

If your stairs squeak because one of the treads is badly split or if the wood is so worn that the tread tends to buckle in the middle, then you should replace the tread as soon as possible. On a staircase that is open on the underside you can make a temporary repair by screwing one or more wood blocks or braces to the underside of the tread. However, if the staircase is inside the house where the underside is not exposed, then a professional carpenter should replace the tread completely.

REPAIRING RESILIENT FLOOR TILES

Removing a damaged floor tile (asphalt, vinyl, vinyl-asbestos or cork) and replacing it with a new one is not an exceptionally difficult job—providing you have or can obtain new tiles that match. That's why it is a good idea to buy a few extra tiles whenever a new floor is being installed. Store these where you can find them if and when the need for a patch job ever arises.

The trick in removing one or two floor tiles from the middle of a floor is to do the job without causing damage to the tiles next to it. With most tiles (except for asphalt tile) the only tools you'll need are a sharp utility knife or hooked-blade linoleum knife, a stiff putty knife and maybe a hammer. Start by scoring the tile two or three inches away from one edge, then go over this score mark or cut repeatedly until the knife has sliced all the way through. Try to make the score or cut mark as wide as possible—in some cases it's best to alternately tip the knife to one side and then the other to create a V-shaped groove— you can then get the tip of your putty knife in to pry the narrow strip off (see figure 96).

V-Groove

Score V-groove with knife.

Force putty knife under—

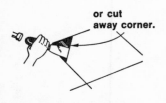

or cut away corner.

Figure 96: **Removing a damaged floor tile.**

Using the putty knife or a chisel and tapping with a hammer if necessary, pry off the strip of tile nearest the edge, then turn the putty knife around and wedge it under the rest of the tile by forcing it under with a hammer. Try to work across the width of the tile so that you remove it in one piece or at least in large pieces if at all possible. Then scrape off as much of the old cement from the floor as you can.

On asphalt tile, and on some older brands of vinyl-asbestos tile, the job will be much easier if you first soften the tile with heat. You can apply heat by working carefully with a blow torch (this is what the pros use) but the simplest and safest technique is to use an ordinary infrared heat lamp or an infrared bulb inserted in a portable lamp or extension cord. Keep moving the source of heat around until the entire tile is warm and pliable, then pry it up carefully by first inserting a utility knife blade along one seam to lift up a corner. A putty knife can then be used to finish the job. If you have trouble getting the corner up, try cutting the corner away first so that you'll have a place where you can insert the blade of your putty knife.

After the old tile has been removed, it is important that you remove most, if not all, of the old adhesive if you want the new tile to lie flat and smooth. Also make certain there is no adhesive around the edges of the adjacent tiles since this will interfere with a snug butt joint.

Before spreading adhesive for the new tile, try laying it down dry first, to make certain it will lie smooth without bumps or irregularities. For best results use the adhesive recommended for that particular brand of tile and spread it on with a serrated spreader (available from any tile dealer) or with a paint brush (if it is the brush-on type). If in doubt as to which adhesive to use, select one designed for vinyl tiles since this will work with almost all other resilient floor coverings. Remember to spread only a very thin layer since putting down too much will cause it to ooze up around the edges and create a messy job. When you set the tile in place, don't slide it—line it up on edge against the adjacent tile, then drop it down flat and press it firmly into place by standing on it. If any adhesive does ooze up wipe it off immediately with a damp cloth.

REFINISHING WOOD FLOORS

When wood floors become so badly worn that the finish is completely gone in some places or if the wood is stained and discolored in many areas, then the only sure cure is a complete refinishing job which involves sanding down to the raw wood and applying a new finish.

If only a few bad spots are visible it is sometimes possible to rejuvenate the floor by scrubbing these areas with steel wool and a liquid floor finish remover or stripping solution, then touching them up with the same finish as the floor originally had (shellac, varnish, penetrating sealer or lacquer). This system works best if the floor was originally finished with a penetrating sealer and wax, since the new material can be applied with a rag and blended in so that it is almost unnoticeable. Chances are you will see a patch to some extent if you're working with shellac, varnish or lacquer.

Sanding Off the Old Finish

When the old finish has to be removed and the floor stripped down to the raw wood, the easiest way to do the job (short of calling in a professional) is to rent a floor sanding machine from your local hardware dealer or tool rental agency. He should rent you two machines: a large drum type sander with its own vacuum bag attached, which you'll use on most of the floor, and a smaller disc type sander which you'll use around the edges and for door saddles, stair treads and similar small spaces.

Before starting the job remove all of the furniture, including pictures, draperies, blinds and shades. This will save much cleaning afterwards since the sanding operation inevitably leaves a fine film of dust over everything in the room. Loose boards should be tightened by driving nails into the joints between the boards (see page 131) and any protruding nail heads in the flooring should be driven down below the surface with a nail set to avoid tearing the sandpaper or damaging the drum on the machine. To keep the dust from spreading, it's also a good idea to close all the doors that lead to that room and to keep as many windows open as possible while you're working.

For the smoothest finish, old wood floors should be sanded three times: first with a coarse paper to remove the old finish and level off the boards, second with a medium paper to remove scratch marks left by the coarse paper and last with a fine grit paper that will give the wood a final smoothing and leave it ready for finishing.

As a rule, the first sanding (with coarse paper) is done at a 45-degree angle to the boards to knock off the high spots and even up the surface. The second and third sandings (with the medium and fine grit papers) should be done parallel to the grain— in other words along the length of the boards. Because the big drum type floor sanders are quite heavy and exert quite a forward pull when in motion, you'll find it helps to take the strain off your back by using an old belt looped around your waist and tied to the handle of the machine while you're working (see figure 97). This will enable you to use your whole body to hold the machine back, rather than letting the pull be exerted only through your arms and shoulders.

Figure 97: **Using a drum sander.**

Tie belt around waist

SAWDUST BAG

DRUM SANDER

Since floor sanders—particularly when equipped with coarse and medium grit papers—cut into the wood very rapidly, you have to be careful to never allow the machine to stop moving while the drum is turning and in contact with the floor. Start the machine while it is tilted back (press down on the handle to do this) so that the drum is off the floor, then lower it and start walking at the same time. That way you'll avoid accidentally gouging grooves or dish-shaped marks into the floor.

Figure 98: **Use a disc sander for corners and edges.**

Do as much as you can with the large drum sander, then finish off around the edges and in the corners with the disc sander (see figure 98). If there are some corners that you can't get into even with the smaller disc sander, then you'll have to use a hand sander or scraper to complete the job in these areas.

After you've finished the sanding, use a vacuum cleaner, a dust mop and plenty of rags to pick up all the dust from the floor as well as from around the baseboards, moldings and other surfaces (you don't want any of this dust to settle on the floors while you're applying the finish).

Selecting the Finish

Assuming that you're starting with wood floors that have been sanded down to the bare wood, there are two basic types of floor finishes from which you can choose: a penetrating sealer that will soak into the wood and leave an "oiled type" finish with little or no surface film on top of the wood, or a surface coating that will form a hard glossy finish on the floor.

If your floors have not been sanded down to the bare wood—merely scrubbed clean or partially sanded—then only a surface finish such as varnish or shellac can be used. Penetrating sealers can only be applied over raw wood, or over floors which have been previously coated with the same kind of sealers.

The penetrating sealer finishes have either a wax, oil or synthetic resin base and they give a dull, satiny finish rather than a gloss. Since they soak into the wood and leave no appreciable surface film, there is no coating that can scratch, crack or peel (deep scratches will dig into the wood itself). Although the finish itself has very little gloss, a moderate gloss can be achieved by waxing and buffing.

You can buy these sealers in transparent form or in a wide assortment of wood-toned colors, varying from pine to dark walnut. Since the tinted or colored penetrating sealers are actually a combination sealer and stain, they are ideal for staining floors to a darker color while at the same time applying a finish. They wear well, have good resistance to staining and discoloration and enable you to easily "touch up" worn areas—you just rub worn spots with steel wool, then re-apply a fresh coat of the same stain-sealer.

If properly maintained by regular waxing and cleaning, a floor finished with penetrating wood sealer can theoretically last indefinitely since there is no building up of heavy layers—excess material is wiped off as it is applied. The sealer (colored or clear) is uniformly and liberally applied with a large paint brush or folded cloth after which the excess is wiped off with dry rags. A second coat is applied in the same way after allowing for the drying time specified by the manufacturer and wiping off excess material from the surface. The final step is applying a coat of paste wax (wait at least two or three days for this), then buffing vigorously, preferably with an electric buffing machine.

Surface coatings are sold under a great many different brand names but they generally fall into three broad categories—shellac, varnish, and lacquer or plastic finishes. All form a hard glossy surface coating with a built-up finish that some manufacturers claim needs no waxing, but if most of these finishes are not waxed periodically they will wear more quickly in areas that get heavy traffic so that complete refinishing of the entire floor will be required that much **sooner.**

Shellac is the oldest and probably still the most popular of the surface coatings. It dries quickly to a clear glossy finish so that you can apply several coats on the same day (you can walk on it within an hour or two) and it darkens very little with age. It's also highly resistant to scratching and abrasion but if spilled water is allowed to remain on the surface for any time it will turn the shellac white.

Floor varnishes also give a very hard glossy finish but they are much more resistant to water damage than shellac. However, varnishes take much longer to dry, requiring several hours between coats. Thus building up a varnish finish may require keeping a floor out of service for several days in some cases. Some varnishes also tend to darken with age but since all varnishes dry more slowly than shellac or lacquer, they are generally easier to apply. In addition, varnish builds up more quickly to a thicker and heavier film than shellac and lacquer.

Synthetic lacquer and plastic finishes give a surface coating which generally will not darken with age and which is highly resistant to staining and water damage. Some take hours to dry, while others will dry almost as quickly as shellac but most will not give as high a gloss. Practically all of them are somewhat thinner in body so that more coats will be required to build up a sheen equivalent to that of a shellac or varnished floor. Some also have volatile solvents with a strong odor that you may find objectionable while they are drying.

GUIDE TO FLOOR CARE

Although maintenance procedures will vary with different types of floors, there are three general rules that apply to the care of all resilient floor coverings or tiles as well as to the care of hardwood floors:

1. Keep the floors properly protected with a thin layer of good quality wax of the type recommended for that kind of flooring.

2. Wipe up spills and dirt marks as soon as they are noticed—and before the spilled material can harden or dry on the surface.

3. Go easy on the washing. Resilient floor coverings (vinyl linoleum, etc.) should be washed no more than absolutely necessary and even then water should be used sparingly. Except in extreme cases, wood floors should never be scrubbed with water; instead they should be cleaned with a special cleaning wax or other non-water-base solution that is sold specifically for this purpose.

Floors of vinyl, asphalt, linoleum, cork or similar resilient materials should be swept daily to remove surface dirt before it can be ground into the surface. When sweeping won't do the trick the floor should be damp mopped with a dilute solution of mild detergent—not with harsh cleaners or scalding hot water. The surface should then be rinsed with clear water, wringing out the mop sufficiently to keep pools of water from accumulating—even if the manufacturer's instructions say that no rinsing is required.

When selecting a wax for the floor, remember that there are two broad categories from which you can choose: waxes that have a solvent base and waxes that have a water base. Both are available in either liquid or paste form.

Some floors can be polished with either type of wax but be certain that the wax is suitable for your floor covering and will not harm the finish. For example, waxes with a solvent base should never be used on asphalt or rubber tile—though they are the best ones to use on wood and cork floors.

All waxes tend to clean as they polish if they are properly applied with a cloth covered applicator. The fresh wax softens up the old wax and loosens up any dirt that may be embedded in it. This dirt is then picked up by the applicator—but cleaning action will only continue if the cloth on the applicator is changed frequently enough to keep it clean. Some combination wax-cleaners also contain special detergents or other cleaning agents mixed in with them to help remove dirt from the floor as they are applied.

Your wood floors are best maintained by periodic application of a solvent-based wax—a damp mop or sponge should be used only when it is necessary to remove a specific stain or mop up a spill. Under normal use one of the polishing waxes (those that must be buffed) will generally stand up longer than the self-polishing kind.

When, through neglect, a wood floor or resilient tile floor becomes so dirty and stained that simple waxing or damp mopping no longer cleans the surface, then chances are that so much dirt has become embedded in the wax that you'll have to use a liquid wax remover to strip off all of the old wax first. Follow the manufacturer's directions as to how to use this solution, then allow the floor to dry thoroughly and apply a thin coat of fresh wax as soon as possible. Self-polishing waxes are easier to apply but they cannot be buffed between waxing and they may, in some cases, be harder to remove if and when a complete stripping job is required.

CHAPTER IX

FURNITURE REPAIRS

Even though you may never plan to tackle the job of completely refinishing or rebuilding a piece of furniture, there are times when you'll find it necessary or desirable to make some minor repairs yourself, such as mending a wobbly chair or table, fixing a sticky drawer or touching up a damaged finish—either because the job is too small to make it practical to call anyone in or because you just can't get someone to come in and do the work when you want them to (or the price he wants is so high that you decide you will have to do it yourself if you want to get the job done).

This chapter will describe how to tackle some of the frequently encountered furniture problems which are simple enough for you to correct by yourself.

LOOSE JOINTS IN CHAIRS AND TABLES

The best way to repair a loose joint in a wobbly chair or shaky table is to disassemble the piece completely so that you can do a proper job of regluing and reassembling it—especially if the piece has several joints that are loose. As you take it apart, scrape all the old glue off the end of each rung or leg with a dull knife, then apply fresh glue and reassemble the pieces (see figure 99). For most indoor furniture ordinary white glue (the kind that looks milky white in the jar but dries almost clear) will do. For pieces that will take a lot of stress or where more resistance to moisture and dampness will be required, a plastic resin wood glue should be used (this comes in powder form and must be mixed with water before use).

Except where a piece has actually broken or split, joints normally work loose because the wood tends

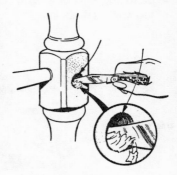

Figure 99: **Scrape out old glue with knife point.**

143

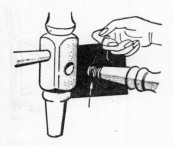

Figure 100: **Wrap the end to be inserted with glue-coated thread to ensure a tight fit.**

Figure 101: **One way to expand the end of a rung or leg so that it fits snugly.**

to shrink and the end of the rung or leg no longer fits snugly in its hole, thus causing the glue to break loose. Remember that wood glues only hold if pieces fit snugly—they will not fill in voids or compensate for poorly fitted joints. Therefore, before reassembling a loose fitting chair leg or rung, it is necessary that you take up the slack by building up the end of the shrunken piece.

There are several ways this can be done but the simplest method is to wrap the end with closely wound linen or cotton thread coated with glue until it fits snugly (see figure 100). Another method that professional furniture repairmen often use is to saw a slot in the end of the rung or leg (as shown in figure 101), then wedge a small piece of wood into this slot to spread the sawed end apart slightly.

Once you've cleaned off all of the old glue and test-fitted the pieces to make certain each fits snugly into its hole or groove, coat the pieces with glue and reassemble them. Some method of clamping or applying pressure is required if you want the glued joint to hold properly and there are various types of wood clamps you can buy for this. On chair legs and large frames you'll find it easier to apply the needed pressure by using a web or band clamp or a simple rope tourniquet which you tighten by twisting with a stick on one side (see figure 102). To keep the rope from cutting into and possibly damaging delicate finishes, use pieces of cardboard where the rope goes around a corner.

On those jobs where you find it impractical to take the piece completely apart, particularly if there is only one loose joint to worry about, you'll have to

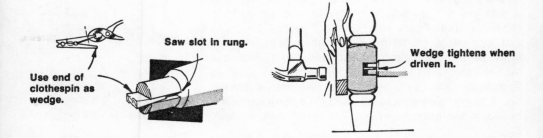

Use end of clothespin as wedge.

Saw slot in rung.

Wedge tightens when driven in.

try and work glue into the crevice around the loose piece. By working gently you can often pry the joint open far enough to permit you to scrape most of the old glue out with a thin knife blade (an artist's palette knife is handy for this job) or by using a very narrow screwdriver, glue can then be forced into the joint with a hypodermic-type glue injector (sold in hardware stores and lumberyards that deal in cabinetmaker supplies) or you may be able to run glue into the joint by positioning the piece so that the glue can work its way in by gravity while you help poke it in with a piece of wire or a flat toothpick.

Stick tightens cord when twisted.

Wrap rope around legs.

Figure 102: Applying pressure so the glued joints set properly.

Another trick which the "pros" often use is to drill a small hole through the back side of the joint (about ⅛ inch) then inject the glue into the cavity through this, using one of the hypodermic tools mentioned above. The little hole which remains can be effectively camouflaged by filling with a matching colored putty stick or wood plastic.

Sometimes a chair or table will get wobbly because the frame against which the upper part of the legs is fastened works loose, particularly in the corners. This can also happen with a table whose legs are only braced near the top. In either case, if you'll turn the chair or table upside down you'll generally find that there are metal braces in the corners with a nut (or wing nut) that locks the leg in place—at least on tables. On chairs there may or may not be a similar metal brace or there may simply be a wooden corner block that serves the same purpose (see figure 103).

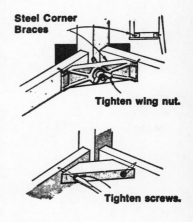

Steel Corner Braces

Tighten wing nut.

Tighten screws.

Figure 103: Strengthening the joint where the frame meets the legs.

Turn the piece upside down and try wiggling the legs around to see where the loose joint is. If the piece has nuts, bolts or screws driven through the edges of the frame, try tightening these with a wrench or screwdriver to make certain that all are secure. If there are wood corner blocks fastened in place with glue you may find that one or more of these joints has broken loose. In this case remove the block completely, scrape off the old glue and replace it with fresh glue and long wood screws. If necessary, also add metal corner irons or corner braces to strengthen the joint where the frame meets the legs.

LOOSE OR BLISTERED VENEER

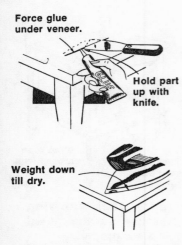

Force glue under veneer.

Hold part up with knife.

Weight down till dry.

Figure 104: **Repairing blisters in veneer.**

When veneer—which is a thin layer of wood—lifts up or blisters on a piece of furniture, it is because the glue that held it in place has crystalized and let loose. To repair it try sliding a knife blade or spatula underneath the raised section, using it as a scraper to clean away as much of the old glue as possible. Or, try working a small piece of sandpaper underneath, pressing down on top of it with the knife blade while you rub. After you're done, blow out any dust or dirt that remains underneath, then work white glue under the loose veneer with the tip of the blade or a cotton-tipped swab (see figure 104).

After you've worked glue over the area, move the loose veneer up and down a few times by pressing on the outside so as to spread the glue around uniformly. Then smooth it down and hold it in place with weights or clamps or even with long strips of adhesive tape wrapped around the corners of the piece. Excess glue that oozes out should be wiped away while still damp so that you don't mar the finish on the surrounding area.

If a piece of veneer is missing entirely or if bad splits are visible after you've glued the loose parts down, you may be able to patch the area with a matching colored wood plastic (sold in most paint stores). However, if the patch is sizable, the lack of grain in it coupled with the fact that it's almost impossible to match the color exactly, will make the patch very noticeable, particularly if it's in a prominent location. In this case your best bet is to try to make a patch out of a piece of the same kind of veneer.

Veneer is still sold in some lumber yards that cater to cabinetmakers, as well as from several mail order houses who specialize in selling materials to hobbyists and craftsmen in the woodworking field. If you can't find one of these sources of supply for the piece of veneer you need or if you need such a small piece that it really doesn't pay you to buy a large sheet, then you may be able to cut a piece large enough to make the patch you need by "stealing" it from the back of the unit or from an inconspicuous corner where a missing piece would be much less noticeable.

To do this, first cut out a piece of the approximate size you will need by working carefully with a sharp knife or chisel. Then pry this off with a chisel, again working carefully to avoid splitting it. Next trim it to fit into the damaged area by laying it on top and cutting through both the new patch and the damaged veneer pieces at once to ensure a perfect fit (see figure 105). If you work carefully and if you try to match the direction of the grains, you can often do a surprisingly good job of making a patch that will be almost unnoticeable after you finish.

Sand exposed surface to uniform level.

DRAWER PROBLEMS

When a drawer in a bureau or cabinet sticks or rubs each time you try to open it, try to remove it completely and then examine the slides or guide strips on the inside of the cabinet. In many cases there will be dust, dirt or other foreign matter jammed into the guides and this will interfere with free operation of the drawer. If so, clean with a stiff brush or vacuum attachment and apply lubricant to the guides as well as to the edges of the drawer itself. Paraffin (an old candle) works well but the new silicone sprays work better and are easier to apply uniformly (see figure 106).

Figure 105: Follow outlines of patch piece when cutting away damaged veneer.

If lubricating both the drawer and the slides or guides does not do the trick, you may have to do some sanding or planing on those edges where rubbing occurs. Needless to say, it's easier to plane or sand the edge of the drawer than it is the guides, but try to take off no more wood than absolutely necessary. Usually there will be marks to indicate where the rubbing occurs but if not you may be able to determine this by careful inspection while shining a flashlight underneath the partly open drawer.

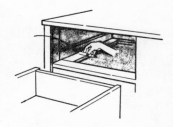

Figure 106: Use bar of wax or candle to lubricate drawer guides.

In some cases binding can also occur because one or more of the guides has worked loose and is no longer in its proper position. You'll see this quickly if you shine a flashlight on the inside to see if any of the guides seems to be out of alignment or if any of the screws or other fasteners that hold them in place is loose. Another thing that can cause a drawer to become balky is when joints in the drawer itself work loose, particularly at the corners. When this

Figure 107: **If chest is not perfectly level, drawers may fail to work properly.**

happens the drawer is no longer square and will not fit smoothly between the guides. To cure this, reglue the loose joints, reinforcing the corners with one or two small brads if necessary, then wrap with rope (as shown on page 145) to form a tourniquet that will apply needed pressure while the glue dries.

On large chests and double dressers the drawers will sometimes fail to work properly because the whole framework of the chest or cabinet is out of plumb—a condition caused by the fact that the floor on which it stands is wavy or uneven so that the legs do not support the chest properly. If you suspect a condition of this kind you can check for it by using a carpenter's spirit level. Laid on top of the chest the spirit level should indicate that the chest is level from side to side as well as from front to back; held against the side or end of the chest it should show that it's standing "plumb" meaning that it is perfectly vertical (see figure 107). If you find that the chest is not standing level or is twisted slightly (indicated by a slope from front to back at one end), then shim up one of the legs by wedging thin strips of wood or heavy folded cardboard under the low side until the top of the chest is level from side to side as well as from front to back.

BURNS AND SCRATCH MARKS

Small scratches which do not go all the way through the finish and into the wood can often be treated or colored so as to make them scarcely noticeable—a procedure simpler than trying to fill them in. In many cases all you have to do is rub with one of the various oil-based furniture polishes or cream type polishes, while in others a colored liquid scratch remover will do the trick.

White or light colored scratches on a walnut finish can often be successfully camouflaged by simply rubbing over the scratch with the meat of a walnut or brazil nut. This will color it to match the original tone of the wood after which you can restore the luster by waxing or polishing. On dark mahogany finishes, light colored scratches can be touched up by carefully applying a little ordinary iodine, using a small watercolor brush or cotton swab. If the iodine is too dark, it can be thinned with rubbing alcohol to lighten it.

For other colored finishes or where neither one of these methods will match the color successfully, you can often buy small bottles of touchup stain in local paint stores. These come in various colors and sometimes include a small brush attached to the cap. If one color is not suitable as is, the different tones can be intermixed to achieve an intermediate tone. As with most other touchups, you should allow it to dry completely, then restore the luster by applying a light coat of paste wax or furniture polish.

Deeper scratches also need filling in to make them less noticeable and this can often be done with wax-base putty sticks or touch-up sticks—sold in various colors in most paint stores. You apply these by rubbing the stick back and forth across the scratch mark until the crevice is filled in, then scrape off the excess around the edges by working carefully with a stiff piece of cardboard or flexible plastic of some kind. The idea is to remove all material outside the crack or scratch, leaving only the compound inside the crevice. When finished, wipe a light coat of paste wax or oil-type furniture polish over the top but avoid rubbing—merely wipe it on and allow it to dry, then buff lightly.

White rings of the kind often left by wet glasses or hot dishes may or may not be removable, depending on how deep they are engrained and on the kind of finish your furniture has. Try wiping with a rag dampened with one of the following solvents, working in this order: denatured alcohol, turpentine, or lacquer thinner. Test each one on an inconspicuous corner of the furniture first, since some finishes will be removed by one or more of these thinners. In each case wipe on lightly and then rub off immediately with a dry cloth. Of the three, remember that lacquer thinner acts like a remover on most finishes and if you rub on too much (and allow it to stay on too long) it will remove the existing finish completely. Work carefully with this material and only use it as a last resort after you've experimented on the back, bottom or side of the piece where any damage that might occur would not be noticeable.

Another trick that sometimes works on white rings is rubbing with a rag dipped into a paste made by mixing powdered rottenstone (available in all paint stores) with a little lemon oil or ordinary mineral oil. This may remove some of the finish and leave the surface dull because of the abrasive action of the rottenstone but you can restore the luster by waxing or polishing after the color is uniform.

Small burn marks of the kind caused by cigarette ashes or matches can almost always be removed and touched up, providing that the damaged area is not very large and the burn did not go into the wood too deeply. If the burn is very shallow and has merely scorched the finish on top, try rubbing with a dry piece of very fine (000 or 0000) steel wool wrapped around one finger tip. Rub carefully on just the scarred area and you may be able to take it off without going all the way through the finish.

Figure 108: **Scrape off a burn mark with a pocket knife, using a back-and-forth motion; then refinish wood as directed in text.**

If this doesn't do the trick or if the burn mark is too deep for this treatment because the finish is scorched all the way through, then you'll have to scrape the finish down to the wood (and possibly into the wood if the wood is also scorched). To do this use a pocket knife or sharp kitchen knife, holding the knife blade at right angles to the surface as shown in figure 108, then rub back and forth with very short strokes while bearing down with moderate pressure. Scrape the scorched material away until all signs of the scar are removed and then rub the spot smooth with a small piece of very fine steel wool wrapped around one finger.

To fill in the slight dent that remains, use a colored wood plastic or filler of the right shade to match your finish, unless the color of the wood underneath is very similar to the color of the finish alongside. If so, all you have to do to build up the shallow depression is apply several coats of varnish—it may take five or six—with a small brush, allowing each coat to dry hard before you apply the next one.

Varnish can also be used even where the color needs darkening if you're handy with tinting colors—just drip a few drops of oil color into the varnish until it is tinted close to the shade of the finish, then build up the depression in the scarred area by brushing on successive coats of the colored varnish as described above for the clear varnish.

CHAPTER X

IMPROVEMENTS FOR THE INSPIRED

Once you have mastered the basic techniques involved in doing the essential home repairs described in this book, it is only natural that you would want to tackle more advanced projects such as making needed (or desired) improvements in your home or apartment.

For example, with the many new and improved products that are so widely available nowadays, there is no reason why you cannot put down a new floor covering of vinyl tiles, put up a new ceiling, or even panel one or more walls in your house.

In many cases the manufacturer of the various materials you will be using—paneling, floor tiles, etc.—will have detailed step-by-step instructions available explaining how to work with and install a particular product. Also, it is refreshing that many lumber yards, hardware stores and other dealers who stock and sell home improvement materials are no longer as scornful of inexperienced do-it-yourselfers and of women as they once were. They understand that you would not be buying their products if you were unable to do the work yourself and many try to encourage your trade by being quite helpful with all kinds of advice and suggestions.

WALL PANELING

Regardless of whether you want to panel a wall because it is hopelessly cracked and bumpy-looking, because you like the no-maintenance features of modern wall panels or merely because you want the look, feel, and texture of paneling, the project is one that you can safely tackle yourself if you are at all familiar with basic carpentry tools and techniques—and if you can be reasonably patient and careful about accurate measuring and cutting. (There's an old carpenter's saying that is especially true of those who work with paneling—"measure twice before you cut once.")

Most of the wall paneling currently being sold for use in homes will fall into one of three major categories: solid lumber or board panels, plywood and hardboard.

To avoid buying more than you need, measure your room carefully and draw lines on the wall where each panel will end so that you can actually determine how much waste you will have and whether or not the waste pieces will be usable elsewhere. You should make an accurate scale drawing beforehand of your room by drawing each wall separately to indicate where doors, windows, and other openings are, then bring this to your dealer so he can compute the number of panels you will need.

Solid lumber paneling is sold in the form of boards which may vary from four to twelve inches in width and are usually ¾ inch in thickness. There are many variations in style, from tongue-and-groove boards that interlock to square-edge boards that merely butt together. The most popular is knotty pine, but cedar, wormy chestnut, redwood, and other lumber species are also available. Few do-it-yourselfers still install this kind of paneling since there are so many other materials that come in larger sheets or panels which go up quicker and which—being thinner and lighter in weight—are also much easier to install.

Plywood paneling is probably the most popular of all because it combines the beauty of real wood with the convenience of easy-to-install large panels that are comparatively light in weight. In addition, most of the plywood paneling now being sold comes in prefinished form—that is, with a factory-applied stain, sealer and varnish or lacquer so that no further finishing is required after the panels have been installed.

You can buy plywood paneling in all price ranges from inexpensive softwood species to others with a luxurious hardwood veneer such as oak, teak, or walnut. Panels are usually ¼ inch thick and 4 feet wide by 8 feet high but longer panels (up to 16 feet) are also available on special order. Some brands are made with textured or "wire brushed" finishes which give an informal "country" look.

Hardboard wall panels also come pre-finished but in a much wider variety of patterns, colors, and textures, including many realistic-looking plastic-coated wood-grain finishes. They are generally less expensive than comparable quality plywood panels and in addition to the wood grains you can choose from solid colors in a high-gloss or matte finish, imitation tile, marble, leather, exterior siding, and even some with a permanent mural pattern that is suitable for use in bathrooms, dressing rooms, and halls.

Most of these prefinished hardboard panels have a tough plastic coating so that the only maintenance they require is an occasional cleaning with a damp cloth. Some are also available with three-dimensional embossed or textured finishes, including several that give the appearance of outdoor siding, shingles or masonry.

Like plywood, hardboard panels are usually sold in large sheets (4 x 8 feet is the most popular) and they vary from ⅛ to ¼ inch in thickness. Some hardboard manufacturers also make panels in 8-foot long "planks" that are only 16 inches wide—making them even easier to handle when working alone. These are usually installed with special clips that fit into slots in the edge of each "plank" and they are designed so that the slotted edge of one panel overlaps the clips used to hold the adjoining one in place. As a result, you can't see the clips when the job is finished.

Tips on Buying Paneling

When shopping for wall panels remember that no one dealer can stock everything, so if you don't find exactly what you want at one place don't hesitate to look around in more than one lumberyard. Bear in mind that the finishes on prefinished panels vary. Thus a higher priced paneling may be worth the difference because it may have a finish that will last longer. If possible try to see a standard size sample of the actual material rather than ordering from a color card or from a small square of the plywood. Ideally, the best method is to go into the yard and see the full panels before they're delivered since in some cases the sample will differ considerably from the actual material that will be delivered to you—but, naturally, this isn't always possible.

When buying plywood paneling remember that you're dealing with a natural wood product, so don't be surprised if all panels are not exactly the same shade or grain pattern—this is part of the beauty of real wood. When you're buying prefinished hardboard with a wood grain finish you can expect an almost perfect match except for the artificially simulated variations that are created on each panel.

If possible, arrange to have the panels delivered to your house a couple of days ahead of time, then store them in the room where they will be installed so that they will become acclimated to the temperature and humidity in that room and thus minimize the likelihood of warping or buckling later on.

Pointers on Installing Paneling

If the existing walls are reasonably smooth, dry, and not falling apart, then you will be able to mount your new panels directly against the wall without first having to put up furring strips (these may be 1x2-inch or 1x3-inch wooden strips that are nailed to a wall beforehand in order to provide a level base against which panels can be nailed or glued). If you're putting up panels over bare masonry walls (such as in a basement) or if the plaster on your old walls is badly crumbling or cracked, rough, wavy or uneven, then you will need furring strips.

These are usually put up horizontally by driving nails through the plaster and into studs (the 2x4's inside the wall). As a rule, you nail one horizontal furring strip along the bottom of the wall and another one at the top with intermediate strips spaced at 16-inch intervals. Nails should be long enough to penetrate the plaster and go into the studs by at least 1 inch, and if the wall is very wavy or uneven you'll have to slip thin strips of wood behind the furring strips at various points in order to shim them out and create a reasonably straight supporting surface for the paneling.

Most prefinished wall panels are put up by one of three methods: by using only nails, by using a few nails combined with an adhesive, or by using special clips. The method you will use will depend to a great extent on the type of paneling you select. In some cases the manufacturer will give you a choice—either use nails alone or nails combined with an adhesive. Bear in mind that if you choose to nail the panels up, you'll have the extra chore of hiding the nail holes. In grooved paneling this is not much of a problem since you can usually drive the nails into the grooves (where they'll scarcely show). Where you have a choice, your best bet is the combination nail-and-adhesive method. With this, you use only a few nails across the top to hold the panel in place while the adhesive sets.

The adhesive itself is applied to the back of each panel with an ordinary caulking gun in long ribbons or wavy stripes. Follow the directions on the package as to the amount to be applied as well as the setting time required before you tap the panel permanently into position. The usual method is to apply the adhesive to the furring strips on the wall, then press the panel into place and drive a few nails part way in along the top to act as a "hinge." Now pull the panel out at the bottom so it is a few inches away from the wall and wait about ten minutes for the adhesive to partially set. Then press it firmly back against the wall and use a hammer with a block of wood to tap it into tight contact at all points. The "hinge" nails along the top are then driven all the way in and a few additional nails driven along the bottom (these will be covered by molding later on).

When cutting prefinished panels of hardboard or plywood, keep in mind that if you are using a portable electric circular saw or saber saw you should work from the back side—making your cuts with the face or "good" side down. If, on the other hand, you're using a hand saw then the opposite is true—make your cut with the face side up. The reason for this in each case is if any splintering occurs, the splintering will occur on the back rather than on the face (with a hand saw the cutting action takes place on the downstroke; with an electric saw the cutting action takes place on the upstroke).

Since plywood and hardboard panels are quite thin, in most cases you'll have no problem with the trim around windows and doors as you can get a neat job by fitting the panels carefully against the existing trim. If this causes a problem then it may be better to rip the old trim off and replace it with new moldings that match the paneling (these go on top of the panels).

You can usually fit the paneling against the top of the existing baseboard, but for the neatest and most professional-looking job the baseboard should be pried off before installing the paneling. You can then renail the original baseboard or, better yet, buy matching prefinished molding that will blend in with the new paneling. There are also matching corner moldings, cove moldings (for along the ceilings) and other moldings available to provide a neat, professional look to the finished job.

FLOOR COVERINGS

There is probably no segment of the home-improvement industry that has done as much for the do-it-yourselfers as the advent of resilient floor tiles and sheet flooring. Manufacturers of these products have introduced a bewildering array of colorful floor coverings in all price ranges and in every conceivable color and pattern that are easier than ever for an inexperienced person to install.

You can buy tiles which have their own adhesive on the back so that all you have to do is peel off a protective paper backing, then press them into place, or you can buy foam-backed sheet floor covering that can be applied without adhesives of any kind. Patterns vary from smooth glossy solids to realistic-looking textured finishes that resemble brick, wood, cork, marble, and other structural materials. Some can be used over any kind of floor—above or below ground—while others can only be installed on suspended (above ground) floors.

Choosing Your New Floor

Aside from aesthetic considerations of color, pattern, and texture, you'll probably have to consider cost as well as ease of installation and general suitability when shopping for a new floor covering. Bear in mind that textured patterns which are deeply embossed will generally not show scratch marks or scuff marks and will require less polishing and waxing—but they may also be harder to clean because dirt tends to accumulate in the recessed parts of the pattern.

Tiles (squares or rectangles) will always be simpler to install than sheet flooring—but sheet flooring will go down faster with no seams to worry about. Needless to say, the tiles which have their own adhesive on the back are going to be much simpler and quicker to install than those that require spreading an adhesive on the floor. You really don't need a thick, heavy-duty commercial grade of tile in your home—the thinner grades will last as long as you will need them, and they will be much easier to cut, fit, and install (also they cost less).

Pointer on Installing Floor Coverings

Before putting down any floor, remove all of the furniture from that room if possible. For the neatest job it is also advisable to remove the baseboard molding so that you fit the tiles against the baseboard and then replace the molding on top to cover irregularities.

Remember that all resilient tiles will eventually mold themselves to the contours of the flooring beneath them, so make sure the subfloor is as smooth as possible. In most cases if you have old tile on the floor that is still in good condition, you can lay new tile over it—but for specific instructions on this you'll have to check with your dealer or with the manufacturer of the tile (there are some that recommend removing all old tile first).

If the old floor is wood, remove or fix any protruding nails or loose boards and remove high spots or rough spots by sanding or planing where necessary. Wood plastic or wood putty (a powder you mix with water) can be used to fill in large cracks or splits. In extreme cases, if the boards are badly cupped or warped or if all the joints are open so that patching is impractical, you'll have to put down a subfloor of hardboard or plywood first. You can buy this material in 4-foot squares from most floor covering dealers and you put it down with special coated nails that will prevent "popping" later on.

Concrete floors in basements or enclosed patios should be swept clean and cracks or worn spots patched with a latex patching cement. Remember that on basement floors you can't lay tile if the concrete has been painted—unless one of the newer latex (water-thinned) deck paints was used, and this is at least 6 months old before you lay tile over it. If the floor has a solvent-thinned (turpentine) deck paint on it, all the old paint will have to be removed first—either by sanding or by use of a chemical paint remover (unfortunately both methods are messy and time-consuming).

When the old floor has been properly prepared by patching and cleaning where necessary, you're ready to start laying your new tiles. As a rule you start in the center of the room and work out toward the walls, rather than the other way around. The reason for this is that few rooms are really square and few walls are really straight, so if you were to start along one wall chances are that by the time you got to the the other end of the wall the line of tile would gradually move away from the baseboard so you would have to cut very narrow pieces to fill in.

To locate the center of the room, you measure the midpoint of each wall, then snap a chalk line from one side to the other. Where these lines cross is the center of the room. Before starting to cement the actual tiles in place, lay a row down dry (without adhesive) to see how the pattern will work out as it reaches the wall at each side. If you find that you are left with very narrow strips to fit, then move your center line half a tile closer to the wall that the narrow strips approach and start putting tiles down on this center line instead of on the original one.

After you've spread the adhesive according to the directions supplied you can start setting your tiles in place but never slide the tiles—always push them straight down so that the edge of each one butts snugly against the edge of the one you just laid. Sliding tiles over after they have been pressed down causes adhesive to ooze up between them and will result in a sloppy looking, uneven job.

It's usually best to lay all of the whole tiles first, leaving the pieces around the edges for last. When necessary to fit around pipes, radiators or other obstructions, the easiest method is to make a paper pattern first, then trace this onto the tile and cut to fit. Cut border tiles one at a time, measuring each one separately (or making a pattern for each one separately) and then replace the baseboard molding after you have finished. Remove any smears of excess cement as soon as they are noticed, but wait at least one day before you do any waxing or general cleaning (don't mop with water for at least a week).

PUTTING UP A NEW CEILING

To remodel an old ceiling that is hopelessly cracked, bumpy or flaking, there are two techniques you can follow. You can paste ceiling tiles directly against the old ceiling or you can install a suspended ceiling which consists of panels supported on a metal grid that is hung below the existing ceiling.

Cementing tiles against the existing ceiling is the quickest and easiest method and will only lower your present ceiling by the thickness of the new tile plus the adhesive used to hold it.

Suspended ceilings are hung below the existing ceiling so they can only be installed in rooms which have enough height to permit lowering the ceiling by at least 6 inches. However, suspended ceilings do have several advantages—for one thing wiring or plumbing can be run overhead above the ceiling where it will be easily and instantly accessible when and if repairs are needed. The individual panels can be easily removed or lifted out when repairs or replacements become necessary, whereas cemented-in-place tiles are quite messy and difficult to remove once they are in place. There is one other advantage to a suspended ceiling; you can include concealed fluorescent lighting fixtures that fit into the same grid opening so that you have a ceiling which gives light as well as acoustical insulation.

Pointers on Installing Ceiling Tiles

Ceiling tiles usually come in 12-inch squares and may have simple beveled edges so that one square merely butts against the other or they may have tongue-and-groove flanges so that the edge of one tile interlocks with its adjoining tile as it is installed. As mentioned previously, when installing them directly over an old ceiling you normally put them up with a special mastic cement or adhesive. A thick dab is applied to each corner of the tile, plus one in the center. Then it is pressed into place. Some brands will also recommend driving one or two staples in through the flange (on tongue-and-groove tiles) to hold the tile in place while the adhesive sets.

On very rough ceilings or when tiles are to be applied directly over exposed joists (as when finishing a basement), ceiling tiles are usually installed by stapling after first nailing up furring strips across the joists. These are 1x4-inch strips of wood which you nail at right angles to the ceiling joists. The strips provide a firm, level foundation against which the ceiling tiles can be stapled. Directions supplied with the tiles will tell you how far apart the strips must be spaced and will suggest when and if they are needed.

Suspended ceilings are not especially difficult to install but the metal supporting framework requires careful measuring and fitting. The first step is to establish your new ceiling height by carefully drawing lines (or snapping a chalk line) on all four walls, using a level to ensure that the lines will be level, rather than depending on measuring down from the ceiling. Metal wall moldings are then fastened to each wall along these lines to outline the perimeter of the new ceiling. The various supporting beams (also made of metal) and cross bars are then suspended across the rest of the room by using the hangers or clips supplied by the manufacturer. On most brands they are hung from the ceiling by driving screw eyes into the ceiling beams, then using pieces of wire to suspend the grid.

Since the metal framing is made of lightweight aluminum it is not especially difficult to work with. Most manufacturers supply detailed instructions on how to lay out and install the supporting grid and all have special clips or locks that simplify snapping the framework together. The individual ceiling panels will then drop in neatly—the only trimming or fitting you'll have to do is around the perimeter of the room where odd-size panel sections will probably be required.

If you plan to include lights in your ceiling, then you'll replace some of the standard acoustical panels with matching translucent plastic panels that are sold for this purpose. It's a good idea to buy these panels, as well as the actual lighting fixtures, at the same time that you buy the rest of the material. In most cases the lighting fixture merely rests on top of the frame, just like one of the panels, with translucent plastic directly under it. Needless to say, you'll have to call in an electrician to do the necessary wiring, but this can be done at any time—either before or after the ceiling has been put up.

INDEX

λ